RUNNING TOWARD THE LIGHT

RUNNING TOWARD THE LIGHT

WILLIAM J. BUCHANAN

WRS
PUBLISHING

A Division of WRS Group, Inc.
Waco, Texas

First published in the United States of America in 1994 by WRS Publishing, A Division of WRS Group, Inc., 701 N. New Road, Waco, Texas 76710
Book design by Kenneth Turbeville
Jacket design by Joe James

Visualtek is a trademark of the Telesensory Company, Mountain View, California, and is used with permission.

10 9 8 7 6 5 4 3 2 1

Library of Congress Cataloging-in-Publication Data

Buchanan, William J., 1926-
          Running toward the light/William J. Buchanan.
                    p.   cm.
          ISBN 1-56796-045-6: $17.95
          1. Mendoza, George, 1955-   . 2. Blind--New Mexico--Biography.
          3. Blind athletes--New Mexico--Biography. 4. Santuario de
          Chimayo (Chimayo, N.M.) 5. Experience (Religion) I. Title.
          HV1792.M46B83 1993
          796.1'96--dc20

                                                      93-45828
                                                      CIP

Dedication

For the Men and Women
of the Special Olympics—
Winners All!

Preface

The genesis of *Running Toward the Light* was a daily diary George Mendoza kept for a brief period following the onset of his illness, and intermittent recordings of events he made over the years soon after they occurred. The bulk of the story is based on extensive interviews with George, his family, close friends, and others who were acquainted with him personally or professionally.

Acknowledgments

In addition to those who appear in this book, I would like to express appreciation to Dr. David Beaver; Gay Clement; Bob Colgan; Max Evans; Norma Fink; Katy Guleff; Dr. Richard Lazaro; Professor Kevin McEvoy; Sister Mary Loyola Muestas; Mrs. Slim Pickens; Father Casamiro Roca; Susan Serna; Irene Trujillo; Isabel Vigil; and others who wish to remain anonymous.

A special thanks to Frank Weimann and staff at The Literary Group, plus the staff of The Authors Guild for their help and support in this and other projects.

—*William Buchannan*

Foreword

I first met George Mendoza, Jr., in October, 1992, when he visited the set of my TV Series, Medicine Woman, at Malibu State Creek Park in California. During a break in filming, we discussed at length his youth, the onset of his blindness at age fifteen, his continued love for running, and a book-in-progress about his life which he hoped would be an inspiration to others who are visually impaired. Like George, and 400,000 other visually-impared persons in America, a very close member of my family is legally blind. I have been a spokesperson for the visually impaired for most of my life. I am a former president of the RP Foundation to Fight Blindness, and, just as George does, I continue in my efforts to raise research funds to improve the lives of those who have been afflicted by visual illness.

The book George and I discussed that day is now a reality. *Running Toward the Light* is the true story of George's long journey back from darkness into the light. I find the book tremendously important—not only for its dramatic impact, but for the indefatigable courage of the man who is its subject. So many of us are tempted to crumble under what we perceive to be unbearable burdens. It's an inspiration and a challenge to read about one who has triumphed over that, and so much more.

—*Jane Seymour*

Chapter
1

Fifteen-year-old George Mendoza tried to focus on the tiny probe light that moved up and down and from side to side in front of him. After a couple of minutes he gave up, frustrated. The doctor switched on the room lights.

"Now, George, look straight at me, please."

George cocked his head in an oblique stare.

"No, George," the doctor instructed. "Into my eyes... look *directly* at me."

The long examination had been exhausting. George said, "Doctor... I *am* looking directly at you."

Across the hall, Lucinda Huber glanced again at the wall clock: 11:15 a.m. She'd been sitting in the waiting room in the Manhattan Eye, Nose and Throat Hospital on East 64th Street in New York since 8:00 a.m. Once or twice she had picked up one of the outdated magazines on the table beside her and flipped through the well-thumbed pages. She was surprised at first to find so many of them printed in extra large type. Then, realizing where she was, she understood. No matter. Her halfhearted attempts to read were fruitless. Her thoughts were on her son.

Cindi (as she preferred to be called) was proud of the job she'd done raising George. He was born at the United States Army Hospital on Governor's Island, New York, on April 1, 1955, when she was twenty-five. Her husband, a private first class, preferred to live off base, so they had leased an apartment on West 105th Street, where he did minor repair work on weekends in exchange for lowered rent. Then, two months after their son was born, Cindi and her husband separated. The separation ended in divorce. Reclaiming her maiden name, she shouldered the responsibilities of parenthood alone. Later, after she moved nearer her parents on Long Island, they and her younger sister, Linda, who was George's godmother, became an extended family to the growing boy. Her parents, owners of the *Three Village Herald*, in Stony Brook, gave her a job on the paper. Linda, a vivacious teenager with an easygoing temperament, took as much interest in her young nephew's welfare as did Cindi, often bragging to friends about George's repeated placement among the top honor roll students at school.

Cindi was equally proud of her son's academic record. Often an unknowing teacher or a casual acquaintance would remark, "You and your husband have done such a fine job raising young George." At such times she would smile and say "Thank you," basking in the inner glow of being a successful single parent.

She was no less proud of George's athletic accomplishments. She had encouraged him to go out for sports in school, wanted him to become involved with male-dominated activity. Tall, like her, but with his father's swarthy Castilian features rather than her Nordic blonde ones, George towered six-feet, one-inch by the time he was fourteen. At Dawnwood Junior High, he took to athletics as if he'd been born for the games, excelling in track, baseball, football, and basketball. With each success came greater acclaim. Cindi delighted in reading about him in sports columns and was thrilled to hear sportscasters predict that upon graduation George Mendoza would have his pick of college scholarships. Whether he was *that* good yet, Cindi couldn't judge. But she knew he was good, and getting better.

Then came that fateful Friday one week before George's fifteenth birthday. In the final basketball game of the season, between Dawnwood and its arch rival, Huntington-Finely, his world began to come apart. Awkward, fumbling, he was unable to hold onto the ball. Twice in free throws he missed the entire backboard. Booed by the crowd, the star center finished the losing game on the bench.

"Mom," he complained later, "the backboard was *swaying*."

He didn't tell her that after the game, when it was time to turn in his uniform, he couldn't find the serial number stenciled on the inside of his shorts, and that a friend had to do it for him.

Cindi insisted that George get a comprehensive medical checkup. The exam took two days. The diagnosis was mononucleosis. The prescription: extended bed rest.

Once during the long convalescence, when Cindi brought his dinner to the bedroom, George stared at the tray, not touching his food.

"What's wrong?" Cindi asked.

"Mom, what's this red stuff on my plate?"

Cindi smiled. She explained that the "red stuff" was lettuce. She dismissed the incident as a result of the poor lighting in the room.

One evening weeks later, sensing George's restlessness from being cooped up so long, Cindi suggested they take a walk. George agreed, eagerly.

A full moon illuminated the village of Centereach that evening. Mother and son walked along an old dirt road to the wooded path George often took to and from school. George stumbled twice, each time grabbing Cindi's arm.

"It's too dark, Mom."

Cindi was puzzled. It was light enough to read a newspaper.

They retraced their steps. At one point along the path a large Colonial house, surrounded by a century-old split rail fence, sat in moon-drenched splendor at the edge of the woods. Cindi surveyed the enchanting scene for a moment, then said, "Just look at that moon, George. You can really make out the Old Man's face tonight."

Silence.

Then: "Mom, I can't see it."

"Right up there. The face is that shaded part..."

"The *moon*, Mom... I can't see the moon."

Oh, Dear God... No! Cindi thought.

In that moment of chilling insight it was all so clear: the fiasco at the ball game, the "red" lettuce, the recent lack of eye contact. Something (for how long now?) had gone wrong with George's vision. Why hadn't she realized it before? She knew why, of course. She'd put complete confidence in the doctors. Not one of them had mentioned an eye problem. Had George truly had mononucleosis? *Eye doctor.* What were they called? An almost debilitating sense of fear gripped her as she led George home. Whatever they were called, she vowed to call a specialist first thing in the morning.

Now, in the waiting room of the Manhattan Eye, Nose and Throat Hospital, Cindi waited for Dr. Peter Rosen to complete his examination of George.

At noon, George emerged from the examination room followed by a slender, shorter man with a receding hairline. George went straight to his mother. "Mom, I've got a rare disease!"

People on adjoining benches turned and stared.

Cindi paled. A *rare* disease?

Dr. Rosen came to where Cindi was seated. "Miss Huber, you have a fine young man..."

Visibly shaken, Cindi blurted, "Doctor... is George going to live?"

"Oh, my! By all means, yes... yes. George, what did you say to your mother?"

"He told me he has a rare disease," Cindi answered.

Dr. Rosen said, "Please, Miss Huber, come with me. George, wait here while your mother and I have a talk."

The walk to his office helped her regain her composure. Now, they sat in facing chairs while Doctor Rosen explained. "Miss Huber, I assure you that George's affliction is not life-threatening. But it *is* serious. You must prepare yourself for what that's going to mean in his life and in yours. It's called 'fundus flavimaculatus.' It's extremely rare. There have been less than a hundred cases reported worldwide, predominantly among young persons. It affects both sexes. It may be hereditary."

Hereditary?

Cindi thought hard. Had she passed this dreadful thing on to her son? There were no serious visual problems in her family, she knew of none anywhere in the Huber generations. Then she remembered. George's father had a cousin who suffered a blinding disease at puberty just as it had now struck George. It was an explanation. But the prospect that it wasn't *her* genes that were responsible didn't make the reality of her son's fate any less disressing.

For the next fifteen minutes, Dr. Rosen explained in lay terms what the tiny, crescent-shaped lesions he had found in both retinal layers of George's eyes meant.

As the ophthalmologist talked, an almost forgotten incident replayed in Cindi's mind. One evening George, then nine, didn't return from a beach party at sundown as promised. An hour passed, then another. As the dark night closed in, Cindi's fears mounted. She decided to go search and picked up the phone to call her sister, Linda, to help. At that moment George came stumbling through the door, sobbing. His clothes were torn, his face was bleeding. Cindi slammed down the phone, led him to a couch, and calmed him. He told her what had happened. He was walking home through the woods when a dank, impenetrable fog encompassed him. Unable to see, he tripped over a boulder and slid into a deep ravine. Afraid to move, he lay there for two hours. When the fog finally lifted, he struggled out of the ravine and ran all the way home.

Late that night George cried out in his sleep. Cindi rushed to his room. He was sitting up in bed, blanket clutched to him, shivering uncontrollably. He was crying. "I... I dreamed... I was *blind.*"

She sat on the bed and drew him close. "Shush. It was just a nightmare. There's nothing to worry about... nothing at all..."

Now, as Doctor Rosen paused in his explanation, Cindi asked point-blank, "Doctor, is George going blind?"

The doctor chose his words with care. "The prognosis is for continued deterioration. As time passes, George will perceive less and less light. Eventually he will lose his central vision and some peripheral vision. He will be legally blind. He'll require special visual aids. After awhile, the need for them will become more pronounced."

"Isn't there something that can be done? An operation... anything?"

The doctor shook his head at the inevitable question. "There's no known cure. I'm sorry... very sorry, indeed."

From his tone and countenance, Cindi knew he meant it. Although he was considerably younger than her, she wondered if he had children of his own.

Inwardly, she tried to grapple with this devastating new reality. *Blindness.* Universally the most feared affliction. What had she... what had George done to deserve this? Though she didn't understand it then, her cascading emotions of grief, anger, isolation, hopelessness, frustration, and above all, guilt, were those felt by every loving parent who receives this kind of news about a child. Overwhelmed, she sat staring into space, barely able to listen further.

The doctor was saying something. What?

She pushed conflicting thoughts aside to concentrate on his words. He was talking about special schools, the career opportunities still available to George. "He could never become a watchmaker, for example, or a pilot. Still, there are a great number of professional opportunities open to the visually impaired." He went to his desk and returned with several pamphlets. "Read these carefully. If you have any questions, anything at all, call me anytime."

Cindi placed the pamphlets in her purse. Straining at the

words, she asked, "Doctor, does George know?"

The doctor nodded. "He's a very mature young man. He asked me to explain it to you."

He rose. "Now, I need to see George again for a few minutes. I'll send him out just as soon as we're through."

She went down the hallway to the rest room and bathed her face in cool water. The towel rack was on the wall near a window. As she dried herself she spotted a group of young boys across the street shooting baskets. At the sight of the hoop, she began to tremble. She grabbed onto the sill. "He'll never... be able to play... basketball again," she said aloud, her voice breaking under the strain.

She was startled by a voice from behind her. "Are you all right?"

She turned. A slender brunette woman about Cindi's size and age was looking at her. She was wearing the white jacket of a medic. Cindi just stared, unable to speak, unable to control her tremors.

The woman placed a hand on her shoulder. "I think you'd better come with me."

She led Cindi to an office much like Dr. Rosen's. Noticing the framed diplomas mounted on the wall, Cindi asked, "Are you a doctor?"

"Yes."

She had Cindi sit on the couch near her desk. Instead of sitting at her desk chair, she sat on the couch beside Cindi. "Now, tell me what's wrong."

Finding her voice, Cindi told this unexpected benefactor about George and Dr. Rosen's bleak diagnosis. "I just don't know... if I can handle it."

The doctor took her hand. "I am so very sorry about your son. But you must understand that what you're experiencing at this moment is the initial shock of a traumatic new reality in your life. I've seen it before, many times. And I'll tell you this from experience. I've never known a mother yet, who, facing the challenge you are facing now, didn't find the strength to cope. You *will* find a way. It's in your maternal genes."

Somehow, talking to this kind woman calmed Cindi's nerves. She dabbed her eyes and thanked the doctor. "I'd better get back," she said, starting to rise. "George will be coming out soon."

The doctor touched Cindi's shoulder lightly, stopping

her from getting up. "How did you get here?" There was genuine concern in her voice.

"I drove," Cindi replied.

"Well, I don't want you to drive back for a while. Rest here on the couch. I'll go get your son. He'll be in the outer office when you feel up to it."

Closing the door behind her, she left Cindi in the office, alone.

Cindi rested on the couch for a half-hour. When she got up, she found George waiting in the outer office. The kind doctor was nowhere in sight. Cindi left without learning her name, an oversight she would always regret.

They drove home in silence. George sat with his head against the window, eyes closed, deep in his own thoughts. At last he said, "Did he tell you?"

"Yes. Do you want to talk about it?"

"Not now."

By the time they pulled into their driveway on Mark Tree Road in Centereach, the setting sun had rimmed the clouds with a rosy lining. Sunset had always been George's favorite time of day. Often, in summer, he would go to the beach after dinner to sit alone and relish the changing hues and patterns the waning sun cast upon the sand and water. Now, in the fading light, he said, "I'm going to stay out here for awhile."

"Yes... sure." Cindi went into the house.

Long after sunset, George entered the house and headed for his room.

"Are you hungry?" Cindi called from the kitchen.

"No. I'm going to bed."

That night she stared at the ceiling, unable to sleep. What could she do to console her son, to help him bear this terrible verdict and face the dark world this monstrous disease had wrought? At midnight, she rose and went to his room. She opened the door quietly and looked toward his bed.

"I'm awake," he said in the darkness.

She entered the room and sat on the side of his bed. "George... I..." At that moment the moonlight illuminated a small framed plaque above his bed: GOD BLESS OUR HOME. She had made the plaque when George was an infant, had woven red yarn onto a piece of one of his baby blankets and hung it there to protect him from harm.

The woman physician she'd met that day in Manhattan

had assured her that she would find a way to cope. But not now, not at this moment. Suddenly she could hold it in no longer. "Ohhh Goddd! *GODDD!*" she cried out in anguish. She slumped across the bed, sobbing, her body shaking in great racking spasms.

She felt his arms around her. "It's okay, Mom... it's okay..."

She had come to console him, she thought. But it was he who was consoling her.

Throughout the remainder of that long night, they wept and prayed together.

Chapter
2

In the forest behind George's home was a path he often took to and from school. Sometimes, after school, he would linger for awhile among the maples and dense scrub oaks to listen to the sounds of the forest, or to watch the birds, or just to think. He didn't mind solitude and found the woods a peaceful escape from his sometimes hectic adolescent world.

It was to these woods that George retreated shortly after dawn the morning after his visit to Dr. Rosen, to try to get a grip on the dark turn of events in his life.

He found the fallen log where he usually sat, scooted up onto it, and leaned back against a tree. Now that he knew what was happening to him, he recalled the clues that had been there all along, although no one had recognized them at the time. It began, as well as he could determine, the day of the big game at school. A day he had so anxiously awaited...

George had but one thing on his mind that blustery Friday in March: the final basketball game of the season that night between Dawnwood Junior High and its arch rival, Huntington-Finley. He always felt pressure before a game, any game—basketball, football, baseball—he played them all and excelled at most. But on that late afternoon, a week before his fifteenth birthday, he left the Dawnwood gym after final practice more worried than usual. There was a new element in his concern, a disturbing problem he couldn't understand.

A sudden gust of wind stirred the dust of the empty playground, irritating his eyes. He reached for a handkerchief and found he had none.

"Ah, hell!" he exclaimed.

Someone spoke up from close by. "Hey, George... hold on. I wanna talk to you."

George thought he recognized the voice. "Billy?"

"Who else?" Billy Claypool answered. "Can't you see someone right on your butt?"

"I can't see nothing. You got a handkerchief?"

"Nah."

George yanked out his shirttail and dabbed at his eyes. "It's all this crud blowing around. Why don't they plant grass in this stupid place?"

"'Cause the little kids like dirt. You going home?"

"Yeah."

George finished wiping his eyes. "Ah... that's better." He stuffed his shirt tail back in, then jabbed a fist at Billy's shoulder. "Okay, turdface, what's on your mind?"

Billy smiled. For ten years now, ever since George and his mother moved to Long Island from New York City, the two boys had been good friends. They started first grade together, explored the deep Long Island woods together, swam in Smithtown Bay together, spear fished at night for flounder in South Bay together, and, more recently, chased girls together. During those years, while George grew into a sinewy teen, towering over six feet by the time he was fourteen, Billy leveled out to a good foot shorter. While George had become a promising athlete, often chronicled in local sports columns, Billy's highest athletic achievement had been to become an assistant sports equipment manager. Through it all, they remained close friends.

"Let's cut through the woods," Billy suggested.

"Sure," George agreed. It wasn't a shortcut, but they often took the longer way home, preferring the forest and meadow trails to the village streets and sidewalks.

"You seen the starting roster for tonight?" Billy asked as they walked. "Three first-string players benched for injury. You know what that means, don't you?"

"What?"

"It means it's all on your back, that's what it means. If you play good tonight we gotta chance. If you screw up... well, like they say, there goes the ball game."

"You ain't making it any damned easier," George complained.

They walked a while in silence, then Billy asked, "So... what's wrong?"

"What's wrong with what?"

"Don't give me that crap. With *you*, that's what. I been watching you at practice. Man, you look like a third-string sub."

George stopped and gave his friend a quizzical look. "You could tell?"

"I could tell."

"Coach hasn't said anything," George countered.

"He hasn't said anything... yet."

They had reached a low hummock where the trail doglegged back toward the village. Here, the tall maples cast long shadows in the waning sun. Here, an old log, bench-shiny from long years of use as a resting place, lay beside the trail. George sat on the log and massaged his temples. He was beginning to get a headache, a recurring problem lately. For a week now things had been going badly at practice. He was off stride, his coordination was faulty, his unerring accuracy beneath the basket was slipping.

"I don't know," George said. "I can't seem to move like I use to. I've been missing shots. That new play Coach set up... you know, the fast break, guard to forward... I keep screwing it up. I can't hold onto the ball."

This last admission worried Billy most. George's ability to pluck a wayward ball out of the air—basketball, football, baseball—was legendary. Sportscasters were beginning to tout "young Mendoza" as "the kid with glue on his fingers."

Billy asked, "You got a bug or something, maybe? You didn't come to the beach picnic Saturday either. Janet was looking for you. She thinks you stood her up."

"I was tired. I stayed in bed."

"All day?"

George nodded.

"It's a bug, sure as hell. Maybe you oughta go right home and get to bed. Rest up for tonight."

"Yeah," George agreed, standing. "That's what I'm gonna do."

The Dawnwood bleachers were packed that night with fans from both schools who came to watch the final game of the season.

George started as a first-string player. He played defensively, without scoring, without trying for a basket. Each time he got the ball he passed at once, seldom trying to dribble for a more advantageous setup. After ten minutes the coach pulled him out.

Billy Claypool inched along the sideline row of metal chairs to George, handed him a towel, and sat down next to him. "What the hell's wrong with you? You didn't even try to score."

"I know," George moaned. He wiped his face and handed the towel back to Billy. "It feels like I got cement in my shoes."

At the beginning of the second half the game was tied 25–25. George remained benched. The game continued to seesaw. With four minutes left to play, the score tied 40–40, one of the Dawnwood forwards tripped an opposing player and both tumbled onto the floor. The Dawnwood player got up limping.

"Mendoza!" the coach yelled. "In!"

On the first play, the Dawnwood center tipped the ball right into George's hands. A Huntington-Finley guard overtook him, grabbed for the ball, and sent George sprawling.

Foul!

The crowd grew quiet as George lined up his first free shot. The ball arched high and fell through the net without touching the rim. Pandemonium! Dawnwood fans rose to their feet. Dawnwood was in the lead.

The crowd held its breath as George lined up the second shot. Suddenly, the basket began to sway in and out of focus. His head was spinning. *What the hell is happening*?!

He took a deep breath, waited until the basket appeared stationary, and shot. The ball struck the wall behind backboard. Huntington-Finley fans cheered. Dawnwood fans moaned. Some booed.

On the next play, Dawnwood recaptured the ball from a startled Huntington-Finley dribbler. George was far down court, close beneath the basket—a sure two points. The Dawnwood teammate threw, George raised his hands to catch. The ball flew straight through his outstretched hands and smashed into his face. Blood spewed from his nose.

From the bench, through tears of pain, George watched the opposing team score two baskets in quick succession. Final score: Huntington-Finley 44, Dawnwood 41. Defeat by three points—the number of points George had a clear opportunity to score, but failed to.

A dejected team filed into the Dawnwood locker room after the game that night. As they prepared their uniforms for end-of-season turn-in, Billy came to where George was undressing. "Man, that was awful! You got about as much chance of making first team next year as I do."

George didn't respond.

As the coach called off players' names, each responded with the issue number of his uniform, stenciled on a tag sewn inside the waistband of the shorts.

"Mendoza."

George fumbled with the shorts, looking for the tag.

"Mendoza! Your number!"

Billy grabbed the shorts from George. "Thirty-two," he yelled, then tossed the shorts back. "For Chrissake, George. Use your eyes!"

Frustrated, George looked again at the shorts. He found the tag, but he couldn't read the number.

He crawled into bed as soon as he got home. He didn't wake up until noon the next day. Stiff, his aching nose swollen and discolored, he rose and put on his exercise suit to make his customary five-mile pre-breakfast run. After ten minutes, his legs turned to rubber. He made it back to the house, back to bed. He remained there the rest of the day.

Cindi regretted that she couldn't attend the game that Friday night. But as a single parent eking out a living for two on a meager income, she needed every penny she could earn. That night, she worked overtime at the paper, proofreading copy for the next week's edition.

By midday, she had heard from others about her son's fiasco on the court the evening before. On her lunch break, she went home to check. He was still in bed, his face a swollen purple mask from his encounter with the basketball. She decided to let him rest.

She had been worried about George for weeks. Last night's game wasn't the first indication that something was out of phase in his life. She had noticed it first in his appearance. His ramrod straight posture had undergone a slight rounding at the shoulders. There were other signs. Always physically active, up each morning for a brisk workout and run, now he would sometimes spend an entire day in bed listening to Beatles records. A brilliant, honor-roll student, he had been reported to the principal twice recently for sleeping in class. Whereas once he'd had a high pain threshold, now he complained of every little ache. Yet whenever she mentioned these things to him, urged him to go to the school nurse for a checkup, he would shrug it off, claiming he was just overtired from a hectic sports season.

She went to her desk, took out her checkbook and studied the balance. Bare bones as usual. No matter. She didn't want to interrupt his semester. But, money or no money, just as soon as school was out, George was going to get a complete physical whether he wanted one or not.

The two-day examination that May was exhaustive. George underwent tests for kidney disease, diabetes, leukemia, blood disorders, liver malfunction, venereal disease, drug addiction, and a host of other possible ailments. All, except a suggestion of anemia, were negative. The final diagnosis was mononucleosis, the prescription was extended bed rest.

Throughout that interminable hot summer, the once fun-filled vacation months of June, July, and August, George remained isolated, confined to bed in his room, or, on occasion, to the living room couch. A voracious reader, he put the first month to use devouring all the books he had put off during school. Among the dozen or so volumes he read those first four weeks, he took the greatest interest in *The Cross and the Switchblade* and *From Ghetto to Glory*. He found those true-to-life stories of faith overcoming adversity exciting, rewarding, and inspirational.

As the summer months ground on, reading became more and more difficult. Television viewing was no better, and his favorite Beatles records soon palled. Other than his family and Billy Claypool, there were no regular visitors. Normally it would have been intolerable. But contrary to the doctor's prognosis, the prolonged bed rest had not improved his stamina. George remained content to lie about, listless, seemingly uncaring.

Then came the night his mother took him for a walk and he couldn't see the moon! That brought things to a head. Frightened, angered at what was surely a wrong diagnosis, Cindi made the appointment for George at the Manhattan Eye Nose and Throat Hospital, where he spent most of the day with Dr. Rosen...

Yesterday, George thought.

The bark of a squirrel sounded nearby. He scanned the trees and spotted the tiny gray animal sitting upright on a branch, high overhead. He watched for a while, wondering how much longer he would be able to see a squirrel—or even a tree! An icy tremor shot through him. How would he ever adjust? How could God, whom he had loved and trusted, allow this to happen to him?

God?

Had he been pressed to reveal the precise time in his life that he began to seek God, he could not have done it. There was no catalyst. His mother, though not indifferent to religion, didn't attend any church. There was no other relative, no churchgoing friend who influenced him. Still, there came a time in his early teens when he began to feel the need for spiritual direction. One night in his room, for no particular reason, he got out of bed, dropped to his knees, and began to pray. Untutored in prayer, he simply poured out his heart to God. Thereafter, he composed daily prayers, often writing them down, often singing them aloud in the woods. Collected into a spiral notebook, these prayers, some simple, some eloquent, became a treasured keepsake.

Now he wondered, Why has God deserted me?

He rose from the log and placed his hands over his eyes and tried to follow the pathway home. His foot became tangled in vines, and he fell headfirst onto the ground. When he sat up he saw that he was at least ten feet off the path, heading into the deepest part of the woods.

He swallowed hard against rising tears. It was no use. He began to cry. Turning his face skyward, he moaned through his sobs, "Oh, God! Help me! Help me!"

It was the last time George Mendoza would call on God for a long, long time.

Chapter
3

To George it was unreal. Unable to come to terms with Dr. Rosen's prognosis, clinging to the hope that the tests were wrong, he entered Centereach High School that fall determined to keep his affliction secret. The result was immediate problems—with faculty, with students, and, predictably, with coaches. George's reputation as an athlete had preceded him. By now, his lackluster performance in the end-of-season game between Dawnwood and Huntington-Finley was considered a fluke. Even the best athletes have off days, it was reasoned.

By the second week of school, when George had not gone near the gym, one of the coaches called him to the locker room. He put an arm around George's shoulder. "I've heard great things about you. I want to welcome you to our squad."

"Nah, I'm not going out for basketball this year," George said.

"Because you're more interested in track, right? Look, no problem, we've got an understanding around here. The track coach and I..."

George shook his head. "Not for track... not for anything."

The coach withdrew his arm. "I think you'd better explain that." It was an order, not a suggestion.

"I'm just not, that's all." George left the locker room.

The incident became the talk of the school. Students, some of them old Dawnwood friends, began to give George the cold shoulder. A few made chiding remarks:

"Mendoza's a fink."

"The Dawnwood hotshot is scared to play with the big boys."

George suspected the stinging taunts were instigated by the coaches to shame him into changing his mind. He'd seen coaches use that tactic before, although he'd always refused to participate.

Predictably, George's classroom work faltered. He could barely make out the print in his texts. He could read the board only if he came early enough to get a front seat.

The first week in math class his teacher asked him to stand and read the problem to be considered that morning. George remained seated. "I can't," he said.

"What do you mean, you can't?" the teacher asked.

"I just can't."

"Do you mean you can't read?"

"I can read. I just can't see well enough today."

"Do you wear glasses?"

George shook his head.

The teacher excused him from class. "Don't come back until your parents buy you a pair of glasses."

George dropped math.

Early one morning, he took a front seat in English class. The room was empty. Ten minutes later it was still empty. George went to the door and cocked his head close to the room number. He was in the wrong room! He rushed down the hallway to the correct room and stumbled into a rear seat, interrupting the teacher's lecture on Shakespeare. When she resumed talking, he was unable to follow the notes she wrote on the blackboard.

At the bell he hurried for the door, just as the teacher called his name. He turned. "George, don't *ever* interrupt my class like that again, do you understand?"

"I..." He started to explain about the wrong room. But how could he do that without explaining why it happened? He said no more.

"George, are you mocking me?"

"Ma'am?"

"Look at me when I'm talking to you!"

It was too much. "Damn it! I *am* looking at you."

He stalked out of the room and went home, skipping the rest of his classes that day.

In the hallway that morning, history teacher Robert Kelly watched George depart in anger. He'd seen all, heard all. He could hardly have missed it. George had almost collided with him in his haste to exit English class. It was as if the boy had not even seen him standing there. For the remainder of that day the discordant hallway scene played in Kelly's mind. He'd been thinking about George Mendoza for days. George was in Kelly's history class. Kelly had watched him fumble with his books and scratch notes in disordered array. Like everyone else at school, Kelly was aware of the smear campaign against the now-reluctant athlete. Surely, something was wrong, something none of them were aware of. Whatever, it had gone on long enough, and he vowed that afternoon to get to the root of George Mendoza's strange behavior.

The next day after history class, Kelly walked over to where George was sitting. "You have a class next period, George?"

"No sir."

"Good. Stick around. I want to talk to you."

When the others had left, Kelly turned one of the front row chairs to face George and sat down. Even sitting, Kelly had to look up at the much taller student. "George, I want to know what's going on."

"What do you mean, what's going on?"

Kelly noted that George's eyes were focused somewhere in space over Kelly's left shoulder. "Cut the crap, George. You know what I mean. Why does a former honor-roll student all of a sudden start failing every class? Why does a first-rate athlete refuse to go out for the team? Why does one of the most popular students in junior high find himself jeered and isolated in high school?"

George shrugged without comment. The gesture irritated Kelly. Then he sensed that George's silence was not defiance, it was resignation. He felt an increasing empathy for this obviously suffering teenager, not much younger than himself.

"George, I'm going to tell you a story."

Without waiting for George's response, Kelly told about a teacher he had in high school. A disciplined instructor, he was nonetheless warmhearted and compassionate, unlike some of the more formidable nuns, brothers, and priests Kelly had for teachers. Kelly learned that he could go to this teacher for advice.

"On *any* problem," Kelly emphasized. "Not just academic ones. He helped me so much with my life, made such an impression on me, that I decided right then that I'd become a teacher myself."

George remained silent. He wondered why Mr. Kelly was telling him all this.

"Know the most important thing he taught me?" This time Kelly waited for a response.

"What?" George asked at last.

"He taught me that unlike a machinist who fashions metal, for example, or a cabinet maker who works with wood, a teacher shapes a human product—a product with feelings and emotions. He taught me that understanding feelings and emotions is just as important as explaining split infinitives or the importance of the Magna Charta." He paused. "I want to help you, George. But I can't unless you tell me what the problem is."

George tried to read Kelly's face. He saw a heavy-set man with reddish-blond hair, matching beard, and compassionate eyes. He decided that Kelly was sincere, not just inquisitive.

"I'm going blind," George said at last.

"Wha... what?!"

Eager now to share the burden, George revealed all in a torrent of words. He told Kelly about the swaying basket in the Dawnwood/Huntington-Finley game, how he was unable see the moon that night with his mother, his increasing inability to make eye contact with another person. Then he told about Dr. Rosen and the grim prognosis for continued deterioration. And how, desperately clinging to the hope that Rosen might be wrong, he had tried to hide his affliction.

Kelly was dumbfounded. He'd suspected a problem at home. Squabbling parents, perhaps, or an alcoholic father or mother, even a divorce in the making. But not this. *A student going blind.* Right under their noses. How could something like this have escaped detection so long? Well, there'd be time for recrimination later. What mattered now was the boy and his future.

"George, you know you've been wrong."

George nodded. "I guess so. I'm... what can I do?"

"You can make a clean breast of things with your teachers and the students. Then we'll... all of us, just have to work things out. And anytime you want to talk, my door's always open. I mean that."

George recognized that it was a sincere offer.

For the first couple of weeks after George's revelation, faculty and students were sympathetic. Coaches quit badgering him. Then, a different kind of reaction set in. Some students became skeptical. To them, blind was *blind.* Yet George moved about without aid, didn't wear dark glasses, didn't use a white cane. George tried to explain that blindness takes many forms. That he was losing his central vision but still had enough peripheral vision to remain mobile. How long that would last, he didn't know.

The skeptics would stare—some would peer intently into

his eyes—then walk away shaking their heads. Their insolence never failed to infuriate George.

Teachers didn't doubt George's affliction. It was confirmed in class every day. He couldn't read, couldn't take notes, couldn't do homework, couldn't take tests. Increasingly frustrated, ever more malcontent, he had developed a don't-give-a-damn attitude. How were they to cope with a student like that? It was disruptive and unfair to other students. However sympathetic one might feel toward him, he was holding back entire classes.

It came to a head in December. One week before Christmas, a faculty committee convened to determine whether George should be permitted to remain in school. That morning, George was called in for a few brief questions, then dismissed. He sensed that things were not going in his favor. He didn't care.

Shortly before noon, he was recalled. Leafing through a file, one committee member said, "George, we're puzzled. We'd like for you to explain why, in spite of your other failures, you're doing well in history."

George wanted to shout: *Because Mister Kelly is the only teacher in this place who gives a damn*!

Instead, he replied, "Why don't you ask Mister Kelly?"

They did.

For the remainder of that noon hour, Robert Kelly educated the educators on how he dealt with George Mendoza. He assigned George a permanent front-row seat; he asked for and got student volunteers to read George's assignments to him; he allowed George to take oral tests; he often spent time after class tutoring George one-on-one; and, occasionally on weekends, he played basketball with George, just to keep the young man involved in life. Kelly emphasized to the board that in his opinion, considering George's recent trauma, he was doing remarkably well.

At the end of the meeting, Kelly emerged from the room and grabbed George by the arm. "C'mon, I'll buy you a burger."

They sat alone in the cafeteria, their sandwiches unwrapped on the tray before them. "They're going to let you stay in school."

"Okay," George said, without enthusiasm.

"Hey, look... you've got to understand, they've never come up against something like this before. But they *are* on your side. The principal has requested that a social worker be assigned to you. We're looking into talking books, optical aids... it's an education for all of us. But we can't do it without your cooperation. Can we count on that?"

The whole matter still rankled. But George knew he owed Mr. Kelly. "Sure. And... thanks."

"Good. Now, eat up before your burger gets cold."

They talked of other things while they ate. But the promise he'd just made weighed on George's mind. He wondered if he'd be able to keep it.

He wondered if he cared.

Chapter
4

Within six months, George lost all his central vision and 80 percent of his peripheral vision. Clinical definitions of blindness range from complete loss of sight to various degrees of residual vision. A person is considered legally blind when central vision is no greater than 20/200 in the better eye. The term 20/200 (Snellen equivalent) means that a visually impaired person can see at 20 feet what a person with normal vision can see at 200 feet. George's Snellen equivalent was 20/400, essentially twice as bad. What a person with normal vision could see at 400 feet, he could see only within twenty feet, and then only by viewing it askance. Beyond the reach of his hands, most colors faded to dull gray. By intense concentration, he could still move about without optical aids, but only on sunny days or in bright light. Even then it was like viewing the world through a handful of soda straws while the focus in each straw constantly changed. On hazy or overcast days he remained indoors. On Long Island, that meant many shut-in hours.

To read he used binocular glasses, a clumsy apparatus akin to goggles with one two-inch-long lens. With the glasses strapped to his head he could laboriously work his way through a text, scanning one or two words at a time. He despised the glasses and used them sparingly.

The most prominent physical change was the discoloration of his eyes. Once a handsome brown, they slowly changed to dull, mottled gray. For Cindi, this gradual destruction of one of her son's most striking features was a constant reminder of the disease that was ravaging him. Struggling to cope, she began to take tranquilizers—secretly, so that George would not learn of her growing dependence on this pharmaceutical crutch.

It wasn't her only crutch.

On weekends and evenings after work, Cindi haunted the libraries on Long Island, researching every book, magazine, and newspaper article that mentioned fundus flavimaculatus. In time, she knew the name of every ophthalmologist worldwide who had researched and/or published papers about the affliction. She wrote to each, asking questions about current research, requesting any new knowledge or treatment. None who responded were encouraging. Undeterred, she began regular correspondence with those who had been most helpful, an exchange of letters that would continue for fifteen years.

During the Christmas season, 1970, Cindi's parents made an announcement: they were selling the *Three Village Herald* and moving.

"Where?" Cindi asked.

"New Mexico," her mother, Belle Jane Huber replied.

It wasn't unexpected. Cindi's father, Bud Huber, had fallen in love with the lower Rio Grande Valley during visits in the 1940s and yearned to retire there. Cindi's job would be secure with the paper's new owners. Linda, too, elected to remain at her job on Long Island.

On Christmas Day, the family gathered for a final holiday feast in the elder Hubers' Long Island home. Over turkey and trimmings, Belle Jane, a sparkling, diminutive lady known affectionately to all as "Nana," described their soon-to-be new home: the mystique of New Mexico's tri-cultural heritage, the incomparable climate of the high plains, the endless azure sky, the multihued desert.

"They call it 'The Land of Enchantment,'" Nana enthused. "It's the mountains that leave one breathless. Great towering peaks, some blanketed with snow the year'round. Truly marvelous sights…"

"Nana…" It was George's voice.

Nana Huber paused in her travelogue. "Yes, George?"

"The mountains… are they big enough for *me* to see?"

Leaden silence. Then Nana moaned, "Oh-h-h-h, George." His plaintive question had pierced her heart.

She rose and went around the table to her grandson and hugged him and gently touched his face. "Yes… yes, my dear. They are indeed big enough for you to see. And you will see them someday. I promise you that."

Chapter
5

At the beginning of the following summer, Cindi read about a camp, opening soon at Center Moriches on Long Island, that was to operate exclusively for handicapped students. Older students, in George's age group, were allowed to pay the required fee under a work/play program. She encouraged George to enroll.

The first weekend of camp he sat alone on a hill overlooking the compound, wondering why he had agreed to come. After awhile, two girls climbed to where he was sitting. One was covered from head to foot in protective clothing.

"Hi," the protectively clad girl said. "I'm Snow White."

George knew from camp talk that the girl was an albino.

Snow White continued: "And this is one of my dwarfs, Dopey. She sees things bassackwards."

"Not *things*," the second girl countered. "*Words*. I see printed letters backwards, sometimes upside down. It's called dyslexia. And my name's Lois."

"Whatever," Snow White said. "She wants to meet you. She thinks you're some sort of celebrity. Are you?"

"Don't mind her," Lois protested. "She's a real nut. My cousin is a sportswriter in New York. He says they called you 'Glue Fingers.'"

"Yuk!" Snow White exclaimed.

Despite himself, George laughed. "It meant I could always hold onto the ball."

Snow White looked at a long indentation in the ground under a nearby oak tree. It was filled with crushed leaves. "They tell me you sleep outside... with the toads and bugs and everything."

"Sometimes," George admitted.

"Then you must be dopey, too."

"I don't think it's dopey," Lois said. "I think it's neat."

Lois was sixteen. In the light of that clear day she was standing close enough for George to make out dimly some of her features. What he could see, he liked. For the first time, he was glad that he'd signed up for summer camp.

Mutually attracted to each other, George and Lois began to schedule their activities together. She had heard from her cousin that George's rare affliction had cost him a promising sports career. She sympathized with him for that. He learned that her neurologist believed that in time she would overcome her affliction. He rejoiced with her for that.

An aspiring actress, Lois assisted the camp's theatrical director, helping organize and stage plays performed by the students. George's duties included supervising the nightly campfire. Before and after chores, they spent their free time together, jogging each morning along the beach, walking in the afternoons through the woods north of camp.

One afternoon as they walked in the woods, a bank of dark clouds moved in from the bay. "Looks like rain," Lois said. "I love rain."

"Yeah." George strained hard against the rapidly failing light, trying to stay on the trail. Unaware, Lois kept up a steady pace.

The first few drops rustled the leaves above their heads. Lois lifted her face skyward. "C'mon, up there," she shouted with glee, "you can do better than that!"

All at once the clouds erupted in a deluge. Thoroughly drenched, Lois gave a hearty laugh. "Hey... I didn't call for a flood! George, we better get back before they... George? George!"

She spotted him sprawled in the mud several feet off the trail. He was trying to get to his feet.

She ran to him. He clutched her outstretched hand. "Lois," his voice betrayed his anxiety," I can't see."

"Oh, George... I didn't think. Here." She helped him to his feet and grasped him by the hand. "Hold on."

She led him through the downpour to the shelter of a gazebo that stood near the edge of camp. There were no chairs, so they sat on the concrete base to wait out the storm.

"You're one muddy mess," she said, wiping the mire from his face and eyes. Then, impulsively, she leaned close and kissed him.

Caught off guard, he recovered fast and threw his arms around her.

Breaking his grasp, she jumped to her feet. "Oh wow! Crazy, huh? Hey... it's let up. C'mon, we better go."

"Now?!" he blurted.

"Now," she said. "Definitely now." She took his hand again. "I'll lead."

Reluctantly, he rose and followed her back to camp.

At campfire the next night, Lois led a young girl to the log where George was sitting. "George, this is Piper. She's in third grade. Piper, this is George, the fellow I told you about."

"The one who jogs with you on the beach?"

"He's the one. George, can Piper sit with you a few minutes while I run an errand?"

"You bet."

Piper had been totally blind since birth. George knew that "totally blind" persons can sometimes detect changing light patterns. The first night at camp, he had learned to build a huge bonfire for the campers who were visually impaired; the bigger the flames the better they liked it. That evening he had built an especially large fire. He lifted Piper to his lap facing the roaring blaze.

The flames soared higher, tinting avid young faces with an amber glow. All at once a swift breeze from the bay carried a shower of sparks toward the campers. Young voices squealed in delight. Upraised hands swatted at flying embers. Then, a cry of fear. One of the embers had struck Piper's cheek. Terrified, she clawed the air, trying to protect herself from an assailant she could neither see nor understand.

George hugged the cowering girl closer. "Hey, Piper... it's all right. They're just sparks. They won't hurt you."

He explained how the wind was blowing the embers around, how the other kids were swatting at them as if they were darting fireflies. Then, as the breeze died and the sparks drifted skyward, he explained how the wind that had blown in from the sea so quickly had returned to where it came from.

Piper thought for a moment. "George, can you catch the wind?"

He was flabbergasted. "No, Piper. I can run *with* the wind. But I can't catch it."

It was a conversation he would recall many times in years to come.

As the summer progressed, George realized that for the first time since the onset of his illness he was enjoying life. And he knew why. Before his blindness, whenever he'd admire a pretty girl, Cindi would tell him that character and personality were as important as good looks. But good looks in a girl were important to him. Now there was Lois, who met both his and his mother's criteria, good character, sparkling personality, and... a fox! That kiss in the gazebo had been more than a friendly peck on the cheek, too. It was an invitation. And it was time he did something about it.

The next night, George asked Lois to stay at the campfire after the others left. "I need someone to help me back to the cabin."

When the festivities ended, she helped him shovel sand onto the fire and tamp it out. Afterward, as she was leading him up the path, he stopped. "Lois, I want to sleep out tonight. Would... would you... stay with me?"

She stood for a long moment, unmoving. Then, without speaking, she led him off the trail and up the hill to the bed he'd made in the earth beneath the oak tree.

Slowly, they dropped to their knees on the crushed leaves. He pulled her closer to him.

"George, have you... have you ever... ?"

"No... Have you?"

"No."

They lay back, side by side. He wasn't sure what to do next, so he decided to kiss her, which he did, long and hard. He began to feel more confident, more passionate, and started to loosen her blouse. She responded to his passion with passion. Then, abruptly, she let out a gasp and pushed him away from her.

"George... no!" She rolled off the leaves and stood up.

He groped for her in the dark. "Lois... for God's sake! What did I do? Please!"

"George... I'm so sorry." She was crying. "It's nothing you did. I just... we just can't. That's all."

He heard her run down the hill. He lay back in anger, frustration, bewilderment. *What the hell happened?*

The next morning, he rose at first light and walked down to the beach. He sat in the sand at the water's edge, letting the waves of a rising tide wash around him. That's where Lois found him, sitting alone at the shoreline. "George, can we talk?"

"You talk," he said without turning around. "I'll listen." It was the first time he'd spoken harshly to her.

"Can you move back some? I don't want to get wet."

He didn't move.

She remained standing behind him, away from the tide. "It's nothing you did, George. I wanted to, as much as you. But, it's... well, both of us. What if I'd gotten pregnant?"

He turned to face her. "Oh, for God's sake, Lois. I'd *marry* you... you know that."

"Yes... I know that. But you, me... we both have something wrong with our eyes. That wouldn't be fair to... a child. Maybe with someone healthy, either one of us could have a healthy baby. But together... It's just too much of a chance to take."

She waded to him and put a hand on his shoulder. "I know I've hurt you. It hurts me, too. I just hope... you understand."

There was no sensible argument against that logic. Though shaken, he nodded. There was nothing more to say. He turned back toward the sea.

The next day, Lois checked out of camp two weeks early.

All that day and night, George lay alone on the hill beneath the old oak. He'd been a fool in a fool's paradise. All the good feelings were sham. He could never have a normal life, a normal relationship with a girl. Because *he* was not normal. His dreams were like the sparks from all those nightly campfires. Born for one bright shining moment, only to perish in the darkness.

The notion intrigued him. Perhaps that wasn't such a bad idea—to perish into the darkness. It would end the burden, the hurting, the anguish.

He bolted upright. What a black thought!

He lay back down and threw an arm across his face and tried to banish evil from his mind.

But the thought wouldn't go away.

Chapter

6

Tormented by Lois's rejection and faced with the apparent futility of his life, by the time school started that fall of 1971, George was obsessed with thoughts of suicide. During study hall periods, he went to the school library, donned the despised binocular glasses, and tediously researched texts and encyclopedias for information on poisons. Misinterpreting his zeal, his teachers were impressed. One, the English teacher with whom he'd exchanged harsh words with the year before, complimented his new spirit of cooperation. "It's the best thing you can do for yourself, George."

"I know," George replied.

One night, lying in bed tuning through radio stations, he came in on the tail end of a public service announcement warning pet owners not to drain their car radiators where dogs and cats could get to the liquid. The sweet taste of antifreeze, the announcer explained, attracted animals. Highly toxic, it would kill any pet that drank it within a matter of minutes.

Sweet taste. Highly toxic. That's the answer, George thought. His mother always kept antifreeze in the garage. For the first time in weeks, he slept peacefully that night, content that he had found a simple and painless way to end his misery.

The following day at school, feigning interest in the neighborhood pets, he asked his biology teacher about the announcement. "Can dogs really die from drinking antifreeze?"

"Absolutely," the teacher confirmed. "But it's not as dainty as that radio plug would have you believe. Antifreeze poisoning can be a slow, painful death. Almost always an animal will experience a long period of convulsions before dying."

George shuddered at the thought. At once, he put antifreeze out of his mind and returned to his research in the library.

One day he came across a magazine article describing carbon monoxide poisoning. Fascinated, he read how victims merely "went to sleep."

That was more like it, he thought. To go to sleep, and not awaken. It would be easy enough to do, late at night, after his mother had gone to bed. She always kept her car keys on a peg board in the kitchen. He'd have to buy some tubing, to extend from the tailpipe through a window. Then, get in, start the engine, and... go to sleep.

Would God be angry?

That sudden thought unsettled him. He'd not had a spiritual upbringing. Yet, when he began to experience a compelling need for God in his life, he bought a Revised Standard Version of the Bible and read it through, studying long into the night after completing his homework. When he finished the New Testament, he began to attend Our Saviour Lutheran Church on Mark Tree Road, within easy walking distance of his home. Over the next three months, to the amazement of his pastors, he completed a Bible study course that usually took three years. In May 1970, with Cindi's blessing, he was confirmed by first communion into the Body of Christ. He was fifteen.

After the onset of his illness, he gave up prayer. Yet he continued to attend church regularly, hoping to detect through the sermons some reason for God's wrath. Then, two things happened in close order that changed the course of his religious convictions.

Unable to see the pulpit, but still able to hear, he changed his seating to a pew where the acoustics were good and listened intently to the sermons. Before services one Sunday, a prominent member of the church council called George aside. "I noticed that you didn't participate in the singing last week, George."

George revealed that he was going blind and could no longer read the words in the hymnal.

The councilman expressed condolences. "It's very distracting to the other members, though. Here's what you should do. Open your hymnal and mouth the words you hear. That would be much better for everyone."

How absurd, George thought.

Nonetheless, that Sunday he tried the suggestion. He felt like a fool. Halfway through the first song he put the hymnal down and never picked one up again.

The following Sunday a visiting bishop based his sermon on Matthew 8:28—the demon-possessed men of Gadarenes. Whether or not the bishop said so explicitly, George understood the message to be that persons afflicted with illnesses were suffering God's vengeance for the sins they had done. It was too much. That Sunday George left the church on Mark Tree Road, never to return.

Now, searching for ways to end his life, George recalled that day. He had left the church. He no longer called on God for help. But would God be angry at what he intended to do? Or would God understand and be forgiving?

He decided it was a risk he'd have to take.

He knew that his mother always filled her car with gas on Sunday, so that it would be ready for the rest of the week. That would be important—a full tank of gas.

On the Sunday before Labor Day, George went to the hardware store in Centereach and purchased eight feet of washer/dryer exhaust vent tubing and a roll of duct tape. He hid the purchase beneath a spreading spirea bush in the backyard. That evening, after dinner, he claimed to have a lot of homework to do. He gave his mother a longer kiss than usual and went to his room. He knew that his mother usually retired early. He lay back on his bed to wait.

In the middle of the night he awakened in panic, barely able to stifle the scream that was rising in his throat. His body was racked with tremors, he was drenched with sweat. He flung his feet over the edge of the bed and sat up. He hadn't meant to sleep.

He'd been plagued by nightmares since the onset of blindness. But this one was the most vivid. Slowly, in his mind's eye, he allowed the hellish dream to replay. He was lying on his back, looking up. High above, faces stared down at him. His mother, Nana, Grandfather Bud, Aunt Linda. They were weeping. *What's wrong?* he tried to ask, but no words would come. He tried to sit up, but couldn't. He reached out to push himself to his feet and gasped—dirt! He was in a grave! The grave began to fill. Spade after spade of dirt rained down on him. He was being buried. But he wasn't dead. He was alive. He clawed at the sides of the grave, desperately attempting to pull himself to the surface. But the soil crumbled in his hands. His body disappeared beneath the dirt. Only his face remained uncovered. He tried to cry out: I'm alive! I'm alive!

I'm alive! he repeated aloud, sitting there on the side of his bed.

He stood and began to pace the room, shivering against

the vivid memory of what he'd dreamed. For the remainder of that night he walked back and forth, replaying the grisly nightmare in his mind, while the message of it seared into his brain. He was alive. And he wanted to remain alive, for as long as God allowed.

On the way to school that morning, he retrieved the sack of tubing and tape from beneath the spirea bush and discarded it in the dumpster behind the gymnasium.

It was the end of all thoughts of suicide.

Chapter
7

As Cindi's research into fundus flavimaculatus failed to produce encouraging results, she felt an increasing sense of guilt that she was also failing her son. Despite assurances from Dr. Rosen and other physicians she consulted, her worst fear now was that George would become totally blind. Clinging to the hope that, somewhere, someone possessed advanced insight into the disease, she intensified her search. It was an exhausting quest. On weekends and evenings, late into the night, and during odd hours she could spend away from her job, she continued to haunt libraries across Long Island.

The project took its toll socially as well as physically. A slender blond in her early forties, with youthful good looks that belied her age, Cindi had no lack of proposals from would-be suitors. Despite admonitions from friends, and, more insistently, from her popular sister, Linda, that she deserved a life of her own, she declined all requests for dates. Driven by George's deepening despair, she devoted herself to finding someone who might offer her son, if not a cure, a least some hope for his future.

In the summer of 1971, while perusing the latest medical journals at Stony Brook University library, Cindi came across an article about Dr. J. Francois of Gent, Belgium. According to the article, Dr. Francois had examined "over forty" patients suffering from fundus flavimaculatus in his research into the disease.

"Forty!" she cried aloud, evoking disapproving stares from other readers.

She smiled an apology at the gawkers and turned back to the article. Forty patients. Out of less than a hundred known cases, worldwide. Certainly, here was the authority she had been seeking.

That evening, more elated than she'd been in months, she wrote a lengthy letter to Dr. Francois detailing the history of George's disease, revealing her fears of total blindness, and asking advice on treatment.

While awaiting Dr. Francois' reply, she pondered another matter that had been on her mind for weeks. She had come across an article about persons who, although not totally blind, suffered severe visual handicaps. One assertion jumped out at her. The article claimed that visually handicapped persons who lived in regions of abundant sunshine were better able to cope with their affliction, both physically and mentally.

How logical, Cindi thought, and berated herself for not having perceived it before. She thought of the dreary, overcast days when George would refuse to venture outside; days when he would turn on every light in the house and leave them on until he went to bed.

She discussed it with Linda. "You know who's constantly bragging about all the sunshine where they live, don't you?"

"Sure," her sister replied. "Nana. You thinking of sending George to New Mexico?"

Cindi hesitated. Then: "I've heard that the reason so many artists settle out there is because colors there are so much more vivid—reds are redder, blues are bluer, so on. I… well, I wonder if George and I should both move there."

Linda feared her sister was not thinking in rational terms. "Have you thought this through?" she asked. "How in the world could you afford to make a move like that?"

Cindi recognized it as an honest question. From the day she and her husband separated, when George was three months old, Cindi had eked out a meager living at best. It had been a traumatic time. There had been hard decisions to be made, perplexing challenges to be faced. But one decision had been immediate and inviolable—under no circumstances would she give up her infant son.

With no marketable skills, for the first few years she managed the apartment house on West 105th Street where she and George continued to live. To keep in force the agreement for lowered rent in exchange for chores, she took over her one-time husband's tasks of maintenance and minor repairs. Each week she collected rents, cleaned and waxed hallways and foyers, fixed windows, unclogged drains, hung doors, and arranged for maintenance of major items.

As George grew into a bright, perceptive child, he sensed his mother's responsibility for the property. Without being asked, he began to share the load. By the age of four he was roaming the premises checking lights that illuminated entryways, hallways, stairwells. A burned-out bulb meant an immediate report to his mother. For each bulb reported, he earned a penny. By age six, the youthful handyman had graduated to doing simple mending chores on woodwork and plaster. This early sense of responsibility and willing, good-natured support from her son was a source of great pride to Cindi.

When George reached school age, Cindi began to feel a new concern. She had been born and raised in Queens and liked the big city atmosphere; indeed, she preferred it to anywhere else she could think of to live. Yet the mounting social problems in New York schools had not escaped her attention. After careful deliberation she decided—as she had done in the past and would again in the future—to suppress her personal preferences in favor of her son's welfare. She decided to move from the city. And she knew exactly where to go.

Her parents, Elmer J. (Bud) Huber and Belle Jane Huber, and teenage sister, Linda, lived on Long Island. The Huber's newspaper, the *Three Village Herald,* served the bucolic villages of Stony Brook, Setauket, and Old Field. Parents and sister welcomed Cindi and George into their midst, and soon she settled into her new job as a secretary/receptionist/ bookkeeper/ad taker and general jack-of-all-trades at the paper. Her salary permitted her to purchase a cheap used car and a small frame house with a large mortgage. She never regretted the move. The exciting new world of forests, beaches, extended family, and rustic villages where the school bus stopped to allow ducks to cross the road was made-to-order for a growing, inquisitive boy. Then, years later, on the night of the basketball game, her tidy little world began to unravel.

With the onset of George's illness, the sparse savings she managed to accrue evaporated in medical bills. Thereafter, it had been a paycheck-to-paycheck existence while mother and son struggled to come to terms with the calamitous turn of events in their lives.

Now, to her sister's befuddlement, she was contemplating another move—this time all the way across the country.

"I've got some equity in the house," she replied to Linda's question. "I'd sell the furniture with it. The car would bring a couple of hundred dollars, maybe more."

"So, you'd walk to New Mexico."

"Buses are cheap."

To Linda, it sounded like a trial balloon, a plea for advice, or perhaps understanding. She recognized her older sister's dilemma. Except for the first few years in New York City, Long Island had been George's life, the only home he knew.

"What does George think of the idea?" she asked.

"I haven't mentioned it to him," Cindi replied.

"Well, you better do that before you get serious. But if you do decide to go, you're not taking any bus. I'll drive you there myself."

That's where matters stood two weeks later when the mail brought a letter from Belgium.

In a short but significant reply to Cindi's letter, Dr. Francois assured her that the change in color in George's iris was not cause for alarm. Nor, he reported, did fundus flavimaculatus cause total blindness. Still, he cautioned, he could not offer an unequivocal opinion about a person stricken with the disease without a full examination. He suggested that George come to see him.

Seated at the kitchen table that afternoon, Cindi read and reread Dr. Francois' letter. Music from George's radio, which he listened to incessantly, wafted down the hallway to the kitchen. As was becoming more and more routine, he had remained in his bedroom all day. The room had become like a prison to him, a private world where she wasn't invited and could not penetrate. She knew he wouldn't emerge from his cocoon until she called him for dinner.

She looked back at the letter. Dr. Francois had calmed her worst fears. But now she faced a new quandary. After months of unflagging research to find someone who might be able to help her son, she had found him—in Belgium!

She went to the living room and placed the letter in a special box in her desk, along with all the others she'd received from doctors over the years. She closed the box with a silent vow: someday, somehow, her son was going to Belgium to see Dr. Francois.

Meanwhile, there was something she could settle now.

That evening at dinner she told George about her thoughts of moving to New Mexico, and why. "I've already talked to Nana. She can help us find a place to live. She thinks I'll be able to find a job without too much trouble. But before I decide, I want to know how you'd feel about leaving here. Be honest."

For a long while he said nothing. Then he pushed his plate aside and went to his room. Moments later he returned holding the GOD BLESS OUR HOME sign that had hung above his bed since infancy.

"We're not taking this to New Mexico," he said.

He tossed the sign into the trash can.

Chapter
8

Las Cruces, New Mexico—"City of the Crosses"—is located in the most sun-blessed region of a sun-blessed state. Situated forty-five miles north of the Mexican border, it is surrounded on three sides by majestic mountain peaks that tower over 9,000 feet into an azure sky. And it was the azure sky that thrilled seventeen-year-old George Mendoza the first day he arrived at his new home on Baldwin Street in Las Cruces in May 1972. For the first time since the onset of his blindness, he saw the color blue.

There were other heartening distinctions between his vision here compared to Long Island. Although his central vision continued to be a kaleidoscope of mixed images, his peripheral vision improved. He could see no further than before, but within that limited twenty-foot range, images were sharper. By cocking his head and concentrating his gaze toward the side, he could follow a sidewalk and avoid objects he had once tripped over—children's toys or a fallen limb. More heartening, on the brightest days, by tilting his head just right, he could make out a dim outline of the rugged peaks of the Organ Mountains framed against the background of a crystalline horizon.

"You *will* see them someday," Nana had predicted that last Christmas dinner on Long Island, two years before.

Now, her prediction had come true.

With improved vision came an improved disposition. One day he came to the City Housing Office, where Cindi had found work. "Mom, I've got a job!"

Cindi was taken aback. She led him to a quite corner. "What are you talking about, George?"

"I heard about it this morning at the post office. BLM has jobs for handicapped people." He explained that he had gone straight to the Bureau of Land Management office that morning and applied. "I start Monday."

"Oh, George... I don't know..."

"Mom," he interrupted, "you've been carrying the whole load. It's time I did my share. There's nothing to sweat.

These jobs are tailored for people like me."

"What kind of jobs?"

"They call it 'recreational aide,'" he replied, with an amused chuckle. "That's a nice name for common laborer. But they drive us out in buses and bring us back when we're finished. C'mon... okay?"

After a moment she leaned over and gave him a kiss.

"I love you."

He knew it was her way of saying okay.

The job consisted of picking up litter from high-mountain campgrounds, removing weeds and brush along access roads, and stacking firewood at intervals along the walking trails. Occasionally, in approved areas where there were no sudden precipices or other dangers, he worked alone. He found the solitude relaxing. In New York, campgrounds were always swarming with people. Here, one could hike the deep ponderosa forests or vast unfenced mesas for miles without meeting another soul. It was a setting to George's liking. He recalled a book he had once read about the trappers who migrated west a century before. Feeling akin to those mystical mountain men of legend, he began to grow a beard.

One morning while he was washing picnic tables, a fellow worker approached him. "Buenos días, amigo."

George paused. "Say what?"

"Ah, don't speak the lingo, huh? Where you from, my coconut friend?"

"New York. What the hell do you mean... coconut?"

The man laughed. "Brown on the outside, white on the inside. There're some like that. No offense, man. I'm Carlos. Boss told me your name. He says you got a seeing problem."

"You might say that."

"Sorry to hear it. Look, I'm Hispanic too. I know my way around out here. Anything I can do to help... just give me a whistle, hear?"

George sensed it was a sincere offer.

For the remainder of the day, he thought about his heritage. Despite his surname he'd never thought of himself as Hispanic. He'd been raised as a Huber, with Huber family traditions. Yet here he was, with a Hispanic name, living in a region steeped in Hispanic traditions, but he considered himself an Anglo. He hoped the contradiction wouldn't cause him trouble.

As he became more familiar with the territory, he resumed

an old practice. He began to run again. On Long Island, training for basketball or football seasons, he had run for miles each day along the beach. Blindness ended that. Now, during lunch breaks, or in the afternoon after he'd completed his chores, he would walk for a short distance across the unbroken mesa, memorizing the terrain. Then he'd turn and retrace the route at a brisk running pace.

One day Carlos was waiting for him at the end of a sprint. "What the hell you doing, amigo?"

George explained that he had been an athlete in school, that running was a natural high he'd had to give up—until now.

"Well, you *better* run high, man," Carlos admonished. "There're rattlesnakes all over this mesa."

Rattlesnakes!

George shuddered at the thought. He considered Carlos's revelation for a moment. "Well," he said at last, "I'll just have to keep the faith that they won't bite me."

He kept running, each time slightly increasing distance and pace. As sluggish muscles hardened, and stamina returned, he felt an exhilaration he hadn't experienced since his glory days on the playing fields at Centereach.

One afternoon toward the end of summer, while clearing brush in the lower foothills of the Organ Mountains, he came upon a fortress-like cluster of large boulders situated near a small stream. The rocks were partially hidden by a dense stand of piñon trees. Curious, he worked his way through the trees, finally emerging through a narrow breach into a rock-sheltered chamber the size of a small bedroom. A thick layer of pine needles covered the dirt floor. Ten feet above, interlocking branches formed a lattice-work ceiling. He lay back on the soft bed of needles and thought about those summer nights two years ago at the camp at Center Moriches when he had slept on a bed of leaves beneath the sheltering oak tree. Visions of Lois filled his mind. He wondered if she had beaten her dyslexia, if she had… found love.

The thought of the pretty girl on Long Island triggered heartache. He sat up and shook his head to purge the memory.

He fixed his attention on the interplay of light and shadow formed by sunbeams filtering through the evergreen boughs. At last, peace of mind returned. From the look of the chamber, he knew that no other person had been here in

years, if at all. Delighted by the discovery, he decided to
keep it his own private place, to tell no one about it. And in
years to come, this secluded hideaway would play more
than one pivotal role in the life of George Mendoza.

It was during these first summer months in Las Cruces
that a pivotal event also played out for Cindi. She began
dating a man she met in her office. At first, it appeared that
she was on the threshold of a new and meaningful
relationship. But as time passed, the friction between her
suitor and George became as thick as a Long Island fog. She
could understand George's reaction. For as long as he could
remember, she had been all he had. Now, he faced the
painful reality of sharing her with someone else. She kept
her fears to herself and prayed that things would eventually
work out well for the three of them.

One evening at her home, while her boyfriend was
watching TV in the living room, she went to the kitchen to
fix dinner. A few minutes later she heard George enter. She
stepped into the living room just in time see her son fall
headlong over a hassock that her boyfriend had kicked into
his path. Unaware that she was watching, the man guffawed.
"No wonder you're blind as a bat, what with that mop
you're wearing. Get a haircut, you faggot."

Cindi could scarcely believe what she's seen and heard.
Blood boiling, she stalked to the front door, threw it opened
and yelled at her boyfriend. "Out!"

Startled, he started to protest. "Hey, look... it was no
big..."

"Out! Now!"

The man gave them both a snide look, then departed.
Cindi slammed the door behind him. She never spoke to
him again.

Still shaking with anger, she helped George to his feet
and checked to see if he was injured.

"I'm okay," he assured her. Then he added, "I guess I've
really... messed up your life, Mom."

"No, George," she replied. "You *are* my life."

It was an incident he would never forget.

That fall, George entered Las Cruces High School. For the
first time since the onset of her son's illness, Cindi took
heart at the start of a new school year. For now, George was
reading with a different machine.

Shortly before they left Long Island, Cindi came across
an article in *Reader's Digest* about a new invention called
Visualtek. A closed circuit TV-like device, the Visualtek
converted wording on typed or written documents to
headline-size letters, enabling many severely visually impaired
persons to read again with relative ease. She called the
manufacturer of Visualtek in Santa Monica, California. She
learned that only a score of the machines had been built so
far. Price: $1,500. Next morning she mailed a certified check
for down payment on a Visualtek, with a promissory note
to pay the rest on installments. She soon recognized it as
one of the best investments she'd ever made. No longer did
George have to rely on the cumbersome binocular glasses;
no longer did she have to read extended homework texts to
him.

Still, her hopes for a new beginning for George at Las
Cruces High were soon dashed.

On the first day of school one of the coaches spotted the
slim, sun-bronzed teenager towering above other students
in the cafeteria line. A few minutes later the coach came to
where George was sitting. "What's your name, young
fellow?"

George cocked his head to see a hefty man wearing a Las
Cruces High letter sweater and a whistle around his neck.
He knew what was coming. "George Mendoza," he answered.

The coach introduced himself. "I'll be looking for you at
basketball practice after class today, George."

Déjà vu. It was Centereach High all over again. "I can't,"
George said. "I'm blind."

"Blind?" The coach sat down at the table. "You trying to
put me on, fellow?" He stuck his face close to George's and
stared into George's eyes. After a moment he uttered "Shit!"
and abruptly walked away.

George's stomach churned. No apology. No, "I'm sorry
to hear it," or, "I'm sorry to have bothered you..." just
"Shit!"

Furious, George pushed his tray aside, got up, and left
the campus.

Cindi had come home for lunch that noon. She was
making a sandwich when she heard the front door slam.
"George?" she called, wondering why he was home.

He came to the kitchen, his face was contorted with
anger. In a voice barely controlled he told her what had

happened. "That does it," he exclaimed. "I'll never go to school again. *Never!*"

He turned and went to his room.

No longer hungry, Cindi shoved her sandwich aside. In New York, the bitter combination of George's deteriorating eyesight plus the usual turbulent teenage issues had created a crisis a day. Though they had taken their toll, she'd become adept at handling them. Now, she faced the first serious challenge since they had arrived at their new home.

She sat in the kitchen for the remainder of her lunch break reflecting on what had happened to George at the school. It wasn't the first time. And it probably wouldn't be the last. Nevertheless, she was convinced that George's only chance for a semblance of a normal life was through obtaining a good education. No way would she let him throw that away if she could help it.

She wondered if she should confront the coach but rejected the idea. In the macho world of sports, she realized, fathers could get away with that tactic. Protective mothers often accomplished little more than bringing ridicule down on their sons.

She decided to let it ride for the moment. Perhaps when George calmed down, he would return to school.

He didn't.

A week later, convinced by now that George was serious in his determination to never return to Las Cruces High, Cindi brought up the subject of education. They were having dinner at the kitchen table. "There's a school for the visually impaired in Alamogordo," she mentioned while they ate.

George made no reply. He ate in silence.

"It's very highly rated," Cindi persisted. "And it's close enough that you could come home weekends."

"Oh, sure," George responded, at last. "A blind school that teaches you how to weave baskets and make brooms. You want me to make brooms the rest of my life, Mom? That's just great."

"Where did you get an idea like that?"

He told her that Carlos had told him about a school for the blind his cousin attended in Juarez.

"He says graduates spend their lives peddling brooms and baskets to gringo tourists in the border towns along the Rio Grande."

"This isn't Mexico, George," Cindi countered. "And it's

not a 'school for the blind,' it's the New Mexico School for the Visually Handicapped..."

"Mom... look..."

"Please don't turn me off, George. Just listen for a minute, that's all I'm asking."

He gave a shrug.

"I've already talked to a counselor there," she said. "They have a regular curriculum. Many of their graduates go on to college—become lawyers, teachers, there are all sorts of professional opportunities."

She had his attention now, and could tell that he was interested. For the next several minutes she told him all she'd learned about the special school in Alamogordo.

She reached across the table and put a hand on his. "You've never been to a school like that, George. Teachers there understand. So do the students. Because they're just like you."

He promised to think about it.

The next morning he came to the kitchen while Cindi was getting ready to go to work. She'd already eaten and had put his breakfast in the oven to stay warm. She gave him a questioning look. He usually wasn't up this early.

"About that school in Alamogordo, Mom... if it means that much to you, I'll give it a try. But no promises. Okay?"

She knew he was doing it for her. She gave him a tight hug. "Okay. But don't worry. You'll never regret it."

Chapter
9

He regretted it from the beginning.

In later years, George would look back on that first day at New Mexico School for the Visually Handicapped (NMSVH) as the darkest period of his life.

NMSVH is situated on thirty-two tree-shaded acres in Alamogordo, New Mexico, between the Sacramento Mountains to the east and White Sands National Monument to the west. The manicured lawns, red brick buildings accented by evergreens, and shrub-bordered drives make it one of the most attractive campuses in the state. The athletic track behind the gymnasium has the look of any training track found at high schools across the nation, with a singular exception: the inner lane of the oval is bordered by a waist-high metal railing which the severely visually impaired athletes hold onto as a guide when racing. Over the years, the old railing has taken on the sheen of burnished brass from hundreds of hands that have trusted it for guidance.

As he sat through the new student orientation that Monday morning in September, 1972, George was seized by a debilitating fear that he was being institutionalized, cut off from outside life like a convicted felon. No longer was he a disabled student in an otherwise "normal" environment. Here, "abnormality" was the norm. It was a losers' world, he mused, where whatever hopes he had for his future, however meager, would be dashed.

That first evening at dinner, overcome with bitterness, he sat alone at a back table, staring at his tray, not eating. He heard another tray slide onto the table and glanced up to see someone pull back a chair and sit down. The newcomer pulled off a floppy, black, ten-gallon hat, dropped it on the floor, and shoved it under the chair with his foot.

"Name's Gibbs," the fellow said. "I'm an inmate here too. My buddies call me T. G. You and I are gonna be buddies, Mendoza." He started to eat.

Brazen little bastard, George thought. "We are, huh?" He made no effort to hide his disdain.

"You betcha ass," Gibbs said. "How come you're not eating? Long time till breakfast."

"I'm not hungry," George replied.

"First day jitters. You'll survive."

Despite his irritation, George was intrigued. Gibbs' benign irreverence, slow drawl, and seedy garb reminded George of the grizzled cowboys he'd seen on TV as a youth. Gibbs was skinny as a bean pole. Stringy dark hair fell down over his ears in assorted lengths, a ragged shirt-tail hung out over his belt, and the cuffs of his jeans were stuffed into a pair of rundown Western boots. He sported a pair of yellow-lens glasses that George would learn he seldom took off, day or night.

"What's your Snellen?" Gibbs asked.

"My what?" It took a moment for the question to register. "Oh... 20/400."

Gibbs let out a low whistle. "And I thought I had it bad. I'm 20/200."

Gibbs was nineteen, two years older than George. In the days that followed he took George under his wing, escorting him around the campus, pointing out the different buildings and classrooms, introducing him to teachers. Of particular interest to George was Gibbs' running commentary on the conglomeration of students at the school—Hispanics, Anglos, Blacks, Indians. Learning of George's interest in Indians, Gibbs described the different tribes represented by students at NMSVH, with commentary on the culture of each.

George was impressed. "You seem to know a lot about Native Americans."

"Hey, man," Gibbs protested, "*I'm* a native American. So are you. These guys are *American Indians*."

George let it pass.

One day in sociology class, Gibbs pointed out two young women seated by the window. "Apaches," he said. "Mescalero tribe."

George was awed. With the typical Easterner's concept of the warrior tribes, he expected the women to be adorned with dogtooth necklaces and scalping knives. Instead, they wore sweaters, skirts, and loafers—as fashionable as any coed at Las Cruces High. In coming days he would learn that the two were also honor students who set the curve in most of their classes. He decided he had much yet to learn about the "Land of Enchantment."

One afternoon, a few days after their first meeting, George encountered Gibbs walking across the campus in his floppy hat, scuffed boots, the ever-present yellow-lens glasses, and floral swimming trunks. George roared with laughter. "Hey, T. G. Where's the party?"

Gibbs replied that he was heading for the indoor swimming pool. "Physed," he explained. "What'd you sign up for?"

"Nothing," George replied. He revealed that he hadn't participated in sports since going blind.

"You're not gonna get away with that here," Gibbs predicted. He started to walk on, then called back, "Sign up for wrestling. I'm team manager. I'll treat you right."

As Gibbs had predicted, George didn't get away with avoiding sports at NMSVH.

Coach Jack Harmon had noted that the new student hadn't registered for any of the physical education programs offered at the school. He called George aside and pointed out that physical education was a required part of the curriculum.

George sensed that this coach was different. Instead of demanding that he dress out at once, Harmon asked if he had some other physical problem that he hadn't divulged. George confessed that his problem had as much to do with insensitive coaches as it had to do his affliction. He told about the humiliating encounters at Centereach and Las Cruces high schools.

Harmon was sympathetic. "It's not going to be like that here, George. Physed *is* a required subject. But you call the shots. Is there an activity you feel most comfortable with?"

George thought back to his days in the mountains that summer, the times after work when he'd mark off a course on the mesa and run to his heart's content. "Maybe track," he replied, "or wrestling."

"Good," Coach Harmon said. "I'm the wrestling coach. See T. G. Gibbs about our schedule. Now, come with me and I'll introduce you to the track coach."

George was surprised to learn that Coach Philip Shapiro was only three years older than he. The young coach greeted George warmly. After a few moments of getting acquainted, Shapiro said, "We're holding our first meet Wednesday afternoon. Why don't you come out and we'll see how it goes."

The first all-male race that November was a cross-country

event traversing the low foothills and valleys just east of the school. The seven-mile course, brightly defined that day under a cloudless New Mexico sky, was bracketed by guides stationed at intervals to keep the visually impaired runners inside well-marked boundaries. Fifteen students dressed out for the race. Although it was billed as exercise instead of an official match, the spirit of competition ran high.

At the starting gun, the runners pushed off at a slow pace, each man concentrating on those segments of the track he could best follow with limited sight. Near the rear of the pack, George eased to one side and fixed his peripheral vision on the edge of the course. He pulled the cord on his oversize running shorts tighter and kept his pace slow but steady. Ignoring his tail-end position, he lagged further and further behind, determined to enjoy the fun, rather than the competition, of running. By the end of the first slow-paced mile he was last in a field of runners that were now beyond his limited range of vision.

Midway through the race, he topped a small hill that was bordered by piñon trees and prairie grass. Just beyond the crest, a shadowy image caught his attention. He stopped and moved toward the edge of the track, where a slender girl about his age was on her knees picking wild-flowers. In the vivid sunlight, he could make out her features well enough to experience a pang of remorse. A pretty brunette, she bore an uncanny resemblance to Lois.

Once again, as he had that summer day in the hideaway he'd found on the mesa, he recalled the deep affection he'd felt for the girl on Long Island. He wondered if he would ever again find someone like her to love. He wondered if he'd ever find *any girl* to love, or to love him.

Lost in reverie, he didn't notice that the girl had stood and was staring at him.

"You startled me," she exclaimed. "I thought they'd all passed. You're *way* behind."

It brought him back to reality. "Look, I'm sorry. You reminded me of someone I know... I mean, I once knew."

He gave a short wave and turned to resume running. At the first step, his waist cord snapped and his running shorts fell down around his ankles. He sprawled headlong in the dirt. He wasn't wearing a jockstrap.

"Oh, no," the girl exclaimed. "Are you hurt?" She stepped onto the track and started toward him.

He scrambled to his feet. Mortified, he yanked his shorts up to cover his nakedness, held them there and took off in a furious sprint. He kept it up until, minutes later, he heard the beat of other runners just ahead.

They must have stopped for a break, he thought. Or is it possible that I've caught up with them? The thought aroused him. He knew from talk around campus that the field that day contained a couple of the best harriers in the school. Could he catch them? Pass them? Why not try? he thought, just for the hell of it.

He stopped and got the broken cord on his trunks retied. Then, fixing his eyes on the side of the track, he took off again, steadily increasing his pace. One by one, like objects viewed through an out-of-focus camera, the forward runners entered his field of vision, then faded as he passed them by. He didn't count them. He didn't know how many remained ahead, if any.

All at once a new sound reached his ears. Up ahead a crowd was cheering. He must be nearing the end. He kicked into his final sprint. Moments later, the crowd standing at the finish line came within view. Maintaining his fierce pace he crossed the line ten yards ahead of the nearest competitor and fell into the arms of waiting spectators.

"You long-legged sonofabitch!" It was T. G. Gibbs' voice ringing in his ear. "You left 'em eating your dust, every damn one of 'em."

George gasped for breath. For a fleeting moment he was on the playing fields of Centereach again—the star athlete, loved by fans, lauded by sportswriters, destined for glory.

Then, abruptly, a sobering thought crossed his mind. What had he accomplished, really? Where was the glory in beating a bunch of blind guys? Guys just like himself.

He threw his arms around Gibbs' shoulders. "Help me outta here, T. G."

For the remainder of that afternoon and night he lay in his room, unable to sleep, replaying the race in his mind. He found nothing in the recollection to bolster his spirits.

The next morning in the dining hall, he halfheartedly accepted the congratulations of fellow students while he maneuvered toward the table where he knew Gibbs would be sitting. Gibbs stood when he approached and pulled back a chair with a flourish. "Take a seat, champ."

George sat. "Cut the bullshit, T. G."

"Come again."

"The blind beating the blind. Big deal."

"Hey, it *is* a big deal. You're hot stuff on campus today, man."

George threw his tray on the table and sat down. "Well, maybe I don't wanna be hot stuff. Maybe I want to rant and rave and curse fate, like everybody else in this snake pit oughta do. Just get off my case, okay?"

Long silence. It was the same sad song George had been singing yesterday when Gibbs helped him to his room. It upset Gibbs then, but to hear the same old refrain this morning made him angry.

He reached over and grabbed George by the chin and turned his face to one side. "See those guys at that table over there, Mendoza? The white guy and black guy sitting together."

George grasped Gibbs' wrist. "Damn it, T. G., you're pulling my beard."

Gibbs removed his hand. George kept his face turned where Gibbs had turned it. He could make out the two men, dimly. "Yeah. What about it?"

"The white guy's Timm Kailey. He's a champion wrestler. Got so many trophies in his room you have to ease in sideways just to sit down. Black guy's Winford Haynes, one of the best runners in the world. He's won six gold medals already in track, and he's just getting started. They're both blind, like you. But they're a hell of a lot different than you, too."

"Yeah? How?"

"They ain't drowning in terminal self-pity... like you are."

Gibbs stood and grabbed his tray. "Think about it, Mendoza." He left George sitting at the table alone.

George smoldered. Gibbs' rebuke had stung him. And angered him. Gibbs was just like all the rest, he thought. It was a bitter revelation. No one understood. None of them *could* understand what it means to be a rising star one day, and a has-been the next.

Leaving his tray and untouched food on the table, he got up and stalked out of the dining hall. He went to his room, threw the few pieces of clothing he'd brought from home in a bag, and left the campus. At a service station near Highway 70 he stood by the pumps asking motorists who stopped for gas if they were heading for Las Cruces. Near noon, he found a trucker who offered him a ride.

Cindi was surprised to hear George's radio when she got home from work that afternoon. The moment he emerged from his room, she knew something was wrong. They sat in the living room while he told her in detail about the race, the silly accolades that followed, the confrontation with Gibbs at breakfast that morning.

"It's over," he exclaimed. "Schools, coaches, the whole lot." He laid his head back on the couch and closed his eyes.

There was a moment of leaden silence. Then Cindi said, "Gibbs is right, George."

George sat up. "Oh, shit, Mom... not you too."

Since George's blindness had been diagnosed, Cindi had avoided directly confronting him over issues involving his blindness, but instinctively, she knew that if she did so now, he would be dependent on her for the remainder of her life. "Yes, George... me too. You *are* drowning in self-pity. I've tried to understand, to help you to cope. Since the day you got sick, everything I've done has been for your benefit. All the sacrifices—my home, whatever life I might have had of my own—I made willingly. Because I was clinging to the hope that somehow I was helping you make a life for yourself."

She was struggling to keep control. "These past few weeks, I've been so encouraged. The new school... it looked like everything was coming together for you at last. Now, here you are, sullen, mad at the world, ready to throw it all away... again."

Tears streaked her face now. "You've got to get a grip on life, George. You've got to help yourself. I can't do it all. I... just... can't." She put her face in her hands.

He emitted an angry moan. Then, jumping to his feet, he screamed, "Damn you and damn your sacrifices! I don't need you to lecture me! I don't need you at all! Go find your stinking life and leave me the hell alone!"

He left the house, slamming the door behind him.

She collapsed in her chair, crying hysterically.

He awoke to the screech of blue jays squabbling in the piñon just above his head. For a moment he was disoriented, then he felt the bed of pine needles and knew where he was. He'd come here many times before—to this secret hideaway he'd found that day last summer. He would come to escape the frenzied world, to dream of being a mountain man, to camp out beneath the stars. In that clear high-mountain air, even he could make out, dimly, those tiny diamonds dotting the inky sky. Before, however, he had brought food and water, prepared for an extended stay. Now, he had neither. He didn't even remember the walk from his home. But he remembered why, and the memory seared him with anguish.

He rose and walked downhill to the small stream that flowed nearby. Behind him, the sun was just beginning to rise above the peaks of the Organ Mountains. He knelt and drank heartily, then removed his clothing and washed. The icy water invigorated him. Clearheaded now, he dressed and sat back on the stream bank to face up to what he'd done. In the course of a few hours he had rejected his best friend, walked away from the only school that ever understood him, and, far worse, cursed his own mother.

Recalling the scene at home, he was engulfed by a deep sense of shame. He couldn't conceive facing life without her. She had been his shield, a rock in the center of the stormy sea that raged around him.

He sat there for hours, remorseful, contemplating what he could do to atone, to get his life back on track. At midmorning he stood and began the five-mile walk back to town. On the outskirts of Las Cruces, he stopped at a 7-11 Store and bought a baloney sandwich and a pint of milk for breakfast. He ate sitting on a curb. Then he walked across town to Highway 70 and began hitchhiking back toward Alamogordo.

He arrived back on campus shortly after noon and went directly to Coach Shapiro's office. The coach was at lunch, but a student aide was at the desk. "I want to sign up for track," George said.

The aide took a ledger from a drawer and opened it. "Which events?" he asked.

"All of them," George replied.

Chapter
10

In June 1973, George and Gibbs graduated from the New Mexico School for the Visually Handicapped with high school diplomas. To celebrate, Gibbs invited George to hitchhike with him to his home in northern New Mexico. It was to be a portentous visit.

Unlike persons with normal vision, who stood with thumbs out alongside the highway, the two solicited rides from drivers who stopped at service stations, convenience stores, or truck stops. In previous times, they would have accepted rides from any motorist going in the direction they were going. Then an incident occurred that caused them to change their tactics.

They had spent a long weekend in southern Colorado during spring break camping along the Conejos River. On the way home, they caught a ride with a rancher who then turned off at a rural road north of Cumbres.

"Far as I go on the highway, fellows." He put them out. "Good luck."

The sky had been heavy with rain clouds all day. Now, as they stood at the remote intersection, it began to pour. It was George's recurring nightmare—lost in the middle of nowhere on a dark day. He could barely make out his hand in front of his face.

"C'mon," Gibbs said.

Holding Gibbs' hand, George followed at a running pace. When they stopped, he could longer feel the rain, although he could still hear it.

"We're under an overpass," Gibbs explained. "Good a place as any right now."

For the next hour they tried vainly to flag down motorists who seemed to speed up on sighting them.

Finally, a car slowed and stopped right beside them. Gibbs could read the marking on the car.

"State cops," he said. "Maybe they'll help us."

The officers turned on the patrol car's warning lights, then got out and approached the two drenched hitchhikers.

"What do you guys think you're doing?" one officer asked.

"Trying to catch a ride home," Gibbs replied. "Been trying for an hour."

"Can't you guys read?" the officer asked.

"Sure we can read," Gibbs replied, a bit too testy for George's tastes. "What of it?"

The officer pointed. "What's that sign there say?"

Gibbs looked where the man was pointing. "What sign?"

"What sign?! *That* sign right there, staring you in the face."

Gibbs looked in vain for the sign. So did George.

George said, "Officer, if there is a sign there, we can't see it. We're from the New Mexico School for the Visually Handicapped. We're both blind."

Skeptical, both officers stepped closer and looked into George's eyes. Gibbs pulled out his wallet and showed them his NMSVH identification card. "What I meant was, we can read if we're real close."

"Well, I'll be damned," one of the officers exclaimed. "Come here, fellows."

He led them right up to a large white sign with black lettering that was posted beside the road no more than thirty feet from the underpass:

WARNING TO MOTORISTS
DANGER AREA
DO NOT PICK UP HITCHHIKERS

Gibbs read the sign to George, then commented, "Hell's belles and hyenas, no wonder people were speeding by like we were a couple of ax murderers or something."

The officers laughed.

They put George and Gibbs in the patrol car and drove them south across the state line to Chama, New Mexico, where they caught a ride all the way back to Alamogordo.

Neither George nor Gibbs ever learned what the "danger area" was in southern Colorado. But from that time on, they never again accepted a ride without first learning where the driver intended to put them out.

On the first leg of the journey to Gibbs' home that June—Las Cruces to Albuquerque—they caught a ride with a trucker. Following introductions, the trucker remarked, "You wouldn't be the George Mendoza who broke all those high school track records, would you?"

Gibbs fielded the question. "He sure'n hell is. Did pretty good in wrestling, too."

"Well, I'll be damned. I got a celebrity in my truck."

George demurred. "I don't know about 'celebrity'."

"He's too modest," Gibbs said. "I made him what he is today, you know." He laughed at the claim.

George gave an inward smile. Gibbs was closer to the truth than he realized.

After returning to NMSVH that fall following his distressing encounters with Gibbs and his mother, George had entered track events with zeal. Under the guidance of Coach Shapiro and others, he began a rigorous training program. In ensuing months, summoning the inner resources he found during that first cross-country race he won so handily, he ran to victory after victory at southwest regional track meets for the disabled. By graduation, he held the school record in the mile, the half-mile, high jump, shot-put, and softball throw.

The trucker said, "My kid's a fan of yours, George. Hey, there's a notepad and pencil in that glove compartment. He'd love an autograph... Oh, I mean... can you do that?"

George knew the man meant could he *see* well enough to do that.

"Sure."

George found the notepad and wrote his name in the sprawling, oversize script he'd developed after blindness robbed him of his once-impeccable handwriting. Being asked for autographs had become a routine experience for him lately. The requests always puzzled him. Still ambivalent about his achievements, he couldn't understand why anyone would want an autograph from a disabled athlete.

T. G. Gibbs lived in the tiny village of Blanco, situated in the picturesque San Juan River Valley in the northwestern corner of New Mexico, near the sprawling Navajo Indian reservation. Moments after introducing George to his family that afternoon, Gibbs took his visitor by the arm. "C'mon, I got a surprise for you."

He escorted George to a small shed behind the house. "Wait here."

Gibbs entered the shed. Moments later there was a roar of a starting motor, then Gibbs emerged from the shed seated astride a red Honda motorcycle. He revved the powerful engine, then throttled back to an idle.

"Who the hell does that belong to?" George asked.

"Who else, man? Me."

George was flabbergasted. "How did you ever get a license to operate a vehicle?"

"License?" Gibbs gave a belly laugh. "You kidding? Who's gonna issue a driver's license to a blind man? Hop on."

Hop on? Is he serious? George wondered.

Gibbs pointed toward the road. Just across Highway 64 was a large open field. That's where he intends to go, George guessed. Well, why not? He jumped on behind Gibbs and gripped the side of the seat.

With another rev of the engine, Gibbs kicked the Honda in gear. Instead of crossing the highway, he turned onto it and sped away eastward with a screech of burning rubber. George's blood turned to ice water. He knew that Gibbs' eyesight was only marginally better than his own. Hair and beard whipped about his face. He could barely make out the blur of the center stripe against the blacktop as it raced past just beneath his feet. Hot tears stung his face. He wondered if they were caused by wind irritation, or if he was crying.

Gibbs began to call out: "Sixty... sixty-five... seven-ty... seventy-five. Hey, George, how you ridin', old buddy?"

Too petrified to answer, George closed his eyes and tightened his grip on the seat.

Fifteen hair-raising miles later, on the outskirts of the town of Bloomfield, Gibbs skidded to a stop in a gravel lot. George heard rocks pelt wood.

Gibbs cut the engine. "It's thirsty outside," he said. "Let's get a cold one?"

George opened his eyes to see that they were parked against the front door of a rustic log-cabin bar. He swung his leg over the bike and jumped off. His clenched fingers refused to straighten. He shook them in Gibbs' face. "You stupid son-of-a-bitch! You could have gotten us killed!"

"Hey, George," Gibbs said, "I think you pissed in your pants."

George reached down. His crotch was soaking wet. "Oh, for God's sake!"

He folded his hands over the front of his pants, rushed into the bar and looked around for the rest room. Spotting a door in the rear marked MEN, he hurried across the floor and entered. Moments later, a loud scream came from the room. George rushed back out, tugging desperately at the zipper on his pants. He was followed by an irate gray-haired woman who was pounding him with a purse every step of the way.

Plagued by the blind spot in his central vision, George hadn't seen the letters "WO" in front of the letters "MEN."

Bar patrons roared. Gibbs doubled over in laughter. Finally catching his breath, Gibbs grabbed the woman's arm in mid-swing and explained the problem.

"Oh?" she said. "No kidding?"

"No kidding," Gibbs assured her.

The woman apologized to George, then laid a five-dollar bill on the counter. "Drinks for these two on me."

For the rest of that afternoon, he and George drank beer on the house. When at last they left, George refused to ride with Gibbs. He caught a ride with a trucker heading toward Blanco.

Each evening after dinner, George and Gibbs would retreat to the shelter of an ancient cottonwood tree on the bank of the San Juan River. There they'd build a small campfire, split a six-pack or two, and talk late into the night. As always, they shared the cost of the beer, but it was George who made the purchase. Long before, Gibbs had explained why he'd singled George out that first day at NMSVH and declared that they were going to be buddies. "Hell, man, with your size and that ugly beard, no liquor clerk's gonna card you."

On the first evening, Gibbs brought up an unfinished matter. "You said you'd tell me someday why you bailed out on me and those girls at the pool that night. I'm still waiting."

It had happened that spring. One night Gibbs shook George awake at 2:00 a.m. "Get up," he whispered, warning George to be quiet. "Got something to show you."

Half asleep, George let Gibbs lead him across the darkened campus to the gym that housed the swimming pool. A side window was cracked open. Gibbs crawled through and helped George to do the same.

"It's skinny-dipping time," Gibbs exclaimed. "Be careful though, we can't turn on any lights."

George knew that Gibbs often slipped into the poolhouse after hours. This was the first time he'd asked George to come along.

Following Gibbs' instructions, George stripped to the buff, then did a belly whopper into the pool. At once he heard two girls giggling, somewhere close by. They swam to where Gibbs and George were standing in the shallow end of the pool. Gibbs made the introductions. "You got groupies, man. They wanted to meet the champion runner. You only get one of 'em. Don't make any difference though, dark as it is."

George recognized the girls' names as students at the school. For awhile the four swam, splashed water, and dunked each other with abandon. Then Gibbs and one of the girls climbed out. "We'll take the mat room," he said. "You two are on your own."

The other girl took George by the hand. "Let's go to the dressing room."

They climbed out and were heading for the dressing room when George stopped abruptly. "No. Look, I'm sorry... really sorry. But, it won't work."

He groped around for his clothes, found them, and left the gym. After that night, though he and the girl had classes together every day, she never spoke to him again.

Now, three months after the incident, Gibbs demanded an explanation. "Those girls thought you were a fag after that. I didn't argue with them."

George chuckled. "I was afraid she'd get pregnant."

He told Gibbs about the night at camp in Center Moriches when he attempted to seduce Lois, and her explanation of why she wouldn't go through with it. "She was right. The odds against two visually handicapped people having a normal kid are pretty high. That's why I stopped."

Gibbs thought about it. "You mean you ain't ever gonna do it?"

"Hell, no, I don't mean that. I mean I'm not gonna stack the odds against my kid. With a normal girl, no vision problems... hey, that's a different ball game."

"Yeah. If you ever find one that'll play."

"Yeah," George agreed. "If I'm ever that lucky."

One evening a couple of nights later, as they watched the blue-green San Juan waters fade to black under a setting sun, George turned glum. Gibbs asked him what the problem was.

"I've been thinking a lot about my dad lately." George replied.

"Did you ever mail those letters, like I said?"

It was a reference to a scrapbook that George had shown Gibbs, filled with letters George had written over the years to his father but had never sent.

George replied, "Nah. Maybe someday. I'd like to make a name for myself first—do something he'd be proud of."

Gibbs opened two more beers and handed one to George. "Man, you're one messed-up dude, you are. Hell, you could make a name for yourself hands down if you'd just take hold. Look at the records you broke already. You didn't even work up a good sweat picking up that half-mile trophy in Texas. You could make a difference for all of us blind guys if you'd just get your ass in gear. You could be a champion, man. Trouble is, you're too damned timid." He emitted a wicked laugh. "Can't even ride a bike without peeing in your pants."

"And you're too damned reckless," George retorted. "It's a miracle they haven't scraped you off the road with a spatula already. Someone up there must be looking out for you."

"Yeah, you might be right." Gibbs turned uncharacteristically solemn. "George, there's something I been wanting to ask you for a long time. Personal, okay?"

"Shoot."

"Do you believe in God?"

George was taken aback. "You serious, man?"

"I'm serious," Gibbs said.

George sipped his beer for a couple of minutes in silence. Then: "I did, once."

He told Gibbs about his relentless search for God as a youth—how he'd read the Bible through before he was sixteen, how he was the first member of his family to join the church.

"Then, I got sick. One of the ministers had the guts to tell me it was God's will. He laid that platitude on me about the guy who mourned that he had no shoes, until he saw a man with no feet. That was supposed to make me feel better."

He gave a mirthless laugh. "One thing I've noticed... people who spout crap like that always have shoes *and* feet. Anyway, after I lost my sight, I wondered what kind of God would do that to a fifteen-year-old kid. That's when I left the church."

Gibbs tossed a piece of wood on the fire. "Man, you don't doubt God. You *blame* Him."

"That's what a shrink at PH told me. 'Course he didn't believe in God either. He had that 'opium for the masses' attitude. Said my search for God was nothing more than a search for the father I never had."

"What's PH?"

"Public hospital, in Maryland. One of Mom's relatives pulled some strings, got me in. They didn't know a damned thing about my disease there, so they made me a guinea pig, pulled all sorts of crappy tests on me. They even wanted to inject some sort of experimental drug into my eyes."

"Say what?"

"That's right. Wanted to shoot it in there with a needle. I told them, No way. So they put me on a bunch of other drugs that didn't do anything but make me depressed."

He was warming to the subject. "I was rooming with a black guy, Scotty. He was in pretty bad shape. Something wrong with his insides. He said he picked up some crud in Vietnam. But the VA wouldn't approve his claim, so he had to go to PH instead of a VA hospital.

"He asked me if I would read to him. I couldn't, so I made up stories to tell him, like I used to do for kids in camp. Sometimes, when he was hurting real bad, I made up stories for him all night long. He said it helped him fight the pain.

"One night Big Mo came to see us. She was a nurse, about the size of a barn, I never did know her real name. Anyway, she told us that the medics there were no better than witch doctors. Said the only thing could cure me and Scotty was the Holy Spirit. Then she prayed over us. Couple of nights later she brought in these little bottles of water, one for Scotty, one for me. Said it was 'Lourdes Water' from that famous shrine in France. Said Scotty should rub a few drops on his chest every night. Told me to dab it on my eyes.

"One day I was out of the room all day for tests. When I came back, Scotty's bed was empty. I asked the shift nurse where he was. 'Oh, he's dead,' she said, like it was no big deal at all. Like the guy'd just gone to the store or something.

"I sat there for a long time staring at Scotty's bed. Then I grabbed that Lourdes water and poured it down the toilet."

"Ain't nobody in your family goes to church?" Gibbs asked.

"Mom, sometimes. She's still clutching at straws. Christmas vacation she took me to a faith healer in Texas. What a sham. The guy called me up on the stage, and he and about a dozen other blowhards up there put their hands on my head and face and started hollering for the Holy Ghost to make everything all right. That was supposed to be the big cure-all. All it did was give me one of the worst headaches I ever had."

Gibbs chuckled.

"Mom's latest kick is a place called Chimayo," George continued. "Some place up near Santa Fe. She read about a church up there where people claim to get cured of all sorts of things."

He snorted in disdain. "Sometimes I think Mom's the one that's blind."

"Hey, come off it, man. You don't know what you're saying now."

In the glow of the fire, George saw Gibbs cross himself. "What the hell's got into you?" he asked.

"Don't knock Chimayo. It's a holy place. Miracles happen there."

George gave a mocking laugh. "Miracles? C'mon, T. G. Get serious. This is your old buddy George you're talking to."

"I am serious, damn it," Gibbs said, sharply. "Quit knocking Chimayo. Got it?"

George was perplexed. "Sure... okay, if it means that much to you. Just forget I said anything about it at all. Okay?"

"Okay."

They grew silent. Gibbs scooted back against the cottonwood and within minutes was snoring. George chuckled. T. G. never could hold his liquor too well.

George opened the last beer and sipped it slowly, trying to get straight in his mind what had happened here this night. Surely, he had seen a side of his friend that he'd never seen before, had never even suspected. Gibbs was one of the most predictable people he'd ever met. Unconstrained, devil-may-care, often profane. Yet, tonight he had revealed a spiritual conviction that was as intriguing as it was puzzling.

After awhile, George rose, filled the empty bottles with water from the river and extinguished the fire. Then he awakened Gibbs and they stumbled back through the darkness to the house.

He put Gibbs to bed and turned off the lights.

"Hey... George."

"Yeah?" George replied.

"You gotta trust the Lord, man. He's the only hope we got... people like us."

"Yeah, sure."

"George."

"Yeah?"

"You oughta go to Chimayo."

George said nothing.

"What you got to lose, man?" Gibbs said. "What you got to lose?"

And he started snoring again.

Chapter
11

On his eighteenth birthday, George qualified for a monthly Social Security disability payment of $214. That fall, with that small stipend to cover living expenses, and a special student scholarship funded by the U.S. Department of Education, he entered New Mexico State University at Las Cruces. Cindi was elated. The son she'd feared might never complete high school was now on his way to obtaining the education she knew to be imperative to his future.

No less pleased was Aunt Linda.

The year before, Linda had taken leave from her job on Long Island to drive Cindi and George to their new home in New Mexico. The trip transformed her life. Captivated by the panorama of mountains, mesas, and endless sky, she returned to New York just long enough to settle her affairs, then moved west to join her transplanted family in Las Cruces.

Although there was a twelve-year difference in their ages, the sisters were genuinely close. From the beginning of George's illness, Linda had been there to share Cindi's anguish, to offer consolation, to give hope. Now, in New Mexico, she resumed the role of confidante, both to Cindi and to George. And it was to Linda that George first revealed his obsession with what had transpired that night with Gibbs on the bank of the San Juan River in Blanco.

It happened a couple of months after school started.

The university was a mile from George's home. He preferred to walk. On the days Cindi offered to drive him in her second-hand Plymouth, he declined. But on the days Linda stopped by to offer him a ride in her new International Scout, he accepted with glee. He was fascinated with the vehicle, even borrowed the owner's manual to study under the Visualtek. At times, when riding in the Scout, he'd complain about the contrast between himself and his friends when they turned sixteen. "They got a driver's license, I got condemned to blindness." Then he'd deplore that he would never know what it was like to drive a car.

One afternoon Linda was waiting at curbside when George got out of class. Instead of driving him home, she took a road that led out of town. A half-hour later they were high above the valley, on the vast unfenced range of sagebrush and cacti that extended for miles in all directions. Linda stopped, cut the engine, and handed George the keys.

At first puzzled, he finally understood. "Hey! You mean it?"

She got out. "Scoot over."

He moved into the driver's seat. Linda jumped in on the passenger side. He found the key slot and started the engine. Shifting into gear, he released the brake and pushed the pedal to the floor. The Scout lurched forward, snapping them backward against the seat. For a moment, he lost his grip on the wheel. He found it again and whipped sharply left then right into a tight figure eight turn. Then, whooping in ecstasy, he careened across the mesa with abandon, knocking over cacti, uprooting sagebrush, flushing terrified jackrabbits from their lairs. Linda held onto the seat belt for dear life.

Twenty minutes later, he pulled to a stop and cut the engine. "Fantastic!"

He sat back in the seat, his face radiant. "Thanks, Aunt Linda. That's the wildest thing I've done since Blanco."

Linda found her voice. "You're welcome. What's Blanco?"

"Blanco... New Mexico. T. G.'s home." He told her about the frantic motorcycle ride down Highway 64 with Gibbs.

"That's just plain stupid," she said.

"Yeah. That's what I said. T. G.'s a strange guy. Hard to peg." He paused. "You know, I've been doing a lot of thinking about him, ever since that visit."

He told her about the discussions he'd had with Gibbs those nights under the cottonwood tree. "One night I told him about Mom's latest pitch, you know... all that baloney about Chimayo. I guess he thought I was being sacrilegious. He came unglued. Crossed himself... started on me like he was a priest or something. Said I was off base knocking Chimayo.

"Man, I never expected to hear talk like that from him... not T. G. Gibbs. It's been bugging the hell out of me ever since. I even dream about it. How can a guy like him have two such conflicting sides to his personality?"

"Oh, I don't think that's too difficult to understand. Lot's of people come across different once you peel away the outer layers. That's the reason shrinks drive Mercedes."

"I guess so."

He paused a moment. "I got a book from the school library about the place, you know. It says miracles happen there every day."

"Chimayo?"

"Yeah." He gave a mirthless laugh. "Some people will believe anything."

From the way he said it, she realized his conflict ran deep. "You know, maybe you should go see for yourself."

"You mean... Chimayo?"

"What do you have to lose?"

"That's the same thing T. G. said. I guess I should do it, for him I mean."

"For your mom, too. It would really make her happy to take you."

"I don't know," he demurred. Then: "Would you take me?"

"Me? Well, sure, if that's what you want. I'll take you both."

He shook his head. "No... just me."

"I don't understand."

"Just me," he repeated. "I don't want Mom hurt when nothing happens up there. And nothing will. I'm just curious. How about it?"

She started to insist that Cindi go too, but on second thought decided not to press it.

"Saturday, early? You explain to your mom."

"Yeah, Saturday. I'll explain."

"Fine. Now, give me those keys. *I'm* driving home."

Chapter
12

The Spanish-speaking village of Chimayo, New Mexico, is situated in a strikingly pastoral setting of orchards, farmlands, and rustic homesteads in the foothills of the Sangre de Christo Mountains forty miles north of Santa Fe. The town is visited by thousands of people every year. The reason for the pilgrimages is *El Santuario de Nuestro Señor de Esquipulas* (The Shrine of Our Lord of Esquipulas)—today more commonly known as El Santuario de Chimayo. The sojourners come to the tiny chapel by car, by wheelchair, on crutches, or on foot, some walking for hundreds of miles, often laboring the final mile on their knees. Most come in fulfillment of a vow, or to pray for a miracle. Reminiscent of the shrine of Our Lady of Lourdes in France, El Santuario de Chimayo has long been portrayed in literature as "The Lourdes of America."

The legend behind El Santuario has many variations. All versions, however, are variations of a singular theme—the discovery of a mysterious wooden cross (some legends say crucifix) in the mud of a dying spring near the headwaters of the nearby Santa Cruz river. The story most often heard is that of Don Bernardo Abeyta.

In the early 1800s, Señor Abeyta settled on lands that were once home to the Anasazi—the "Ancient Ones" who simply disappeared into antiquity. Later, the region was home to the Tewa Indians. From time immemorial, the Indians had brought their sick to bathe in the "sacred" hot springs, which they considered to have curative powers. One day in 1814, so the legend goes, Señor Abeyta (perhaps accompanied by Indians) spotted a crucifix protruding from the oozing mud of one of the springs that was beginning to go dry. Recovering it, he planned to return it to the church in Santa Cruz from where he thought it came. But the crucifix disappeared, only to reappear in the mud of the dying spring. Twice more, Señor Abeyta attempted to return the rood to the church and twice more it disappeared and "returned" to the spring. Taking this as an omen from Heaven, he erected a small chapel on the spot. As word of the "miracle" spread, people began to come to the chapel to pray for deliverance from pain, to see again, to hear again, to walk again. Though the spring eventually dried up, they continued to come, to kneel at the site inside the chapel where the mysterious cross was found, and to rub the dried earth on their afflictions or to mix it with water and drink it. After prayers that often lasted for days, many began to hang their crutches and braces on the wall and walk away on rejuvenated limbs.

By the time George Mendoza and his Aunt Linda visited the area, over 150 years later, El Santuario de Chimayo had evolved into one of the holiest of holy shrines on the North American continent. (Now owned by the Archdiocese of Santa Fe, the chapel still attracts tourists from around the world.)

As they turned off the main highway that Saturday onto the final route leading to Chimayo, George asked Linda to be his eyes. She described the winding high-desert road leading to the town. Along the shoulder, despite the off-season, people bearing backpacks and walking staffs were hiking the final miles toward El Santuario.

Just after entering the town, which reminded Linda of some of the more charming villages she'd seen during visits to Old Mexico, they turned onto a spur road lined with rustic souvenir shops and small cafes. A tenth of a mile down this road was El Santuario.

As usual on weekends, the parking lot was full. Linda found a space near one of the cafes, then guided George across a wooden footbridge bordered by giant elms. The path led through an arched gateway into a flagstone courtyard in front of the church. Just inside the gate, a priest was recounting the history of El Santuario to a group of tourists. Linda and George listened for a moment, then retreated to the side of the courtyard so Linda could describe the site.

The small adobe chapel was in the most enchanting setting Linda had ever seen. She described the ethereal beauty of the little church nestled in a low dale bordered by juniper-dotted hills. The nearby picnic area was shaded by leafy mulberry trees. A shallow, willow-lined stream coursed just downhill from the chapel. Grave markers inside the courtyard, testified to its use as a cemetery. And two ancient bell towers framed the chapel entrance. Here and there around the courtyard and in the adjacent picnic area, other priests were blessing individual supplicants with special needs. Linda described that scene, too.

Covering her head with a kerchief, she led George past the tourists into the chapel. Just inside the doorway, six low steps led downward through the narthex to the nave. Here, fourteen rows of time-worn wooden benches lined the walls on each side of the aisle. The aroma of burning wax filled the air. At the far end of the nave, two shawl-draped women were lighting candles at a large *candelabro* near the foot of a life-size crucifix. Other persons knelt at the benches, or sat in reverent silence, or wandered the aisle studying the priceless paintings and *bultos* (carved figurines) that adorned the walls and the sanctuary behind the altar.

Just inside the railing, to the left of the altar, was a low doorway that had been constructed in an era of shorter physiques. Linda pushed George's head down, and led him through the door into the sacristy. In this narrow room, where the priests adorned vestments before services, the walls were hung with crutches, braces, and canes. Abandoned wheelchairs sat along the base. Here and there, a handwritten testimonial was attached to a prosthesis, certifying that the user had been cured of an affliction in El Santuario.

On the north end of the sacristy, another low door led to a much smaller chamber, no more than eight feet square. Here, prominently situated in the center of an earthen floor, was a shallow hole fifteen inches in diameter. This was El Posito (the well), the most hallowed site in El Santuario, the pit of sacred earth where the mysterious cross was found over a century and a half before.

In this room, too, the walls were covered with photographs of persons beseeching cures, testimonials of those who claimed cures, numerous paintings, *bultos*, and icons. On this day, two women were on their knees before El Posito. One was rubbing dirt from the well on her bare arm. Another was putting dirt into a jar. While George and Linda were scrutinizing the room, an elderly man in obvious ill health entered and knelt before a glass-encased *bulto* of the crucifixion. He began to pray aloud. They stood to one side until he had finished before they returned to the nave.

They sat on a bench near the altar while Linda described the interior of the chapel in detail. George seemed anxious. Linda asked, "Would you like to speak with one of the priests?"

"No. I'm ready to go if you are."

They were almost to the village limits before he spoke again. "Did you hear what that man was saying?"

"Which man?"

"The old man... the one who was praying aloud."

Linda turned toward the main highway. "Not all of it. Why?"

"He wasn't asking ask for a cure. He was thanking God for a long life. Wanted Him to watch over the kids and grandkids he was leaving behind. How 'bout that?"

"I think it's beautiful," Linda said.

"Yeah."

"What did you pray for?" she asked.

"Me? That's rich. I haven't prayed for anything since I left the church. Came close to it once... on the back of T. G.'s motorcycle." He laughed at the memory.

"Then why'd we come all this way?" she asked.

"Hell, you know why. Mom and T. G. They wouldn't have let me rest until I did. Well, I've done my duty. I've visited their holy shrine. And I can't see a damned bit better than I could when we left home."

Chapter
13

The following July, soon after summer semester got underway, George phoned T. G.

"Hey, my *man*," Gibbs exclaimed. "Long time no see."

"Too long," George agreed.

"How come I don't catch your ugly mug in the sports pages anymore?"

"I gave up all that jock stuff, man. I work up enough sweat trying to keep up with algebra."

"Then you're the same damned fool you always were."

Same old Gibbs, George thought.

"I love you, too," he said. "How about let's talk about it under the cottonwood. I got a week off coming up in August. Can you put me up?"

Gibbs sounded jubilant. "Can pigs eat slop? I'll have the Honda tuned and ready to go."

George laughed. "You know where you can stick that thing. Just stock up on beer, okay? You're old enough to buy your own booze now."

"Said and done," Gibbs replied. And they completed plans for a long overdue visit.

The first weekend in August, George took the Greyhound bus to Albuquerque. There was a two-hour layover in the city before the next northbound bus departed for Bloomfield. He decided to have lunch at the station while he waited. At the counter, he remembered that his old classmate, Antonio Sanchez, lived in Albuquerque. After finishing his sandwich, he went to a phone booth, donned his binocular glasses and looked up Sanchez's number. Sanchez, home for lunch, answered on the first ring.

They chatted for a bit about their alma mater in Alamogordo, then George mentioned that he was on the way to Blanco to see T. G. Gibbs.

There was a foreboding silence on the line. Then Sanchez said, "George, haven't you heard about Gibbs?"

"Heard what?"

"Gibbs is dead."

"Dead?! Don't give me that shit, man. I just talked to him the other day. I'm on my way to Blanco to see him right now."

"I'm serious, George. T. G. was killed in an accident over two weeks ago. I can't believe you didn't hear about it."

There was no response.

"George? You okay?"

George had dropped the phone into his lap and was leaning against the side of the booth in shock and disbelief.

"George!"

George heard the faint, urgent voice calling his name and picked up the phone again. "I... I'm still here. Hey, I don't want to believe this. What the hell happened, Tony?"

From what he learned from Tony Sanchez that day, along with news clippings he was able to find later, George was able to piece together the shocking story.

Shortly after midnight, Saturday, July 13, Gibbs, reportedly after an argument with a girl, sped off into the darkness on his Honda. Near Bloomfield, he entered the Navajo Reservation and turned onto an unlighted service road that paralleled an irrigation project under construction. Minutes later, as he approached the intersection of the service road and State Road 44, he apparently detected lights from oncoming traffic. He slammed on the cycle's brakes, locking them. The Honda flipped over on its side, skidded across State Road 44, crashed through a stop sign, continued skidding down County Road 163, and came to rest at a cattle guard 317 feet from where Gibbs first hit the brakes.

Notified by a passing motorist who saw the cycle skid across the paved highway in a shower of sparks, two New Mexico state policemen hurried to the scene. They found Gibbs lying unconscious in a ditch near the cycle. He had sustained massive head and facial injuries. Although the accident report filed with state police headquarters stated that he was not wearing a helmet, one was found within a few feet of where he lay.

Paramedics rushed him to the San Juan Hospital for initial treatment. Next day he was transferred to Bernalillo County Medical Center in Albuquerque. For five days he clung to the threads of life. But his wounds were too severe. At 7:13 p.m., Wednesday July 17, 1974, Tinney Gray Gibbs died.

In later years, whenever George reflected on that spur-of-the-moment telephone call that noon in the Albuquerque bus terminal, he would suffer an agonizing sense of guilt. For five days his best friend had hovered between life and death, and George had not known about it, had not been at his bedside to hold his hand, to comfort him, to share the suffering.

George caught the next bus back to Las Cruces. He had the driver let him off at the city limits, then walked cross-country to his private hideaway. All that night he mourned in solitude, forfeiting sleep, while he pondered his all-too-short relationship with Gibbs. Flamboyant, irascible, lovable T. G. Gibbs, who scoffed at his handicap—and had been destroyed by it. For the first time in years, George wept for a person other than himself. During that tearful reminiscence, one scene kept playing in George's mind—Gibbs' surprising declaration of faith that night by the campfire on the banks of the San Juan River.

Shortly after dawn he made a fateful decision.

He completed the long walk back to town in two hours, arriving at his home after Cindi had gone to work. He gathered up some camping equipment he'd once used on Long Island, then scrawled a note to his mother at the kitchen table.

Thirty minutes later he was riding northward with a trucker on Interstate 25, en route to Chimayo.

Chapter
14

He arrived in Chimayo at two o'clock that Sunday afternoon with a backpack, sleeping bag, and $2.15 in his pocket. Counting his money, he recalled his one-time minister's pronouncement to the congregation in Centereach: "The Lord will always provide."

"Okay, Lord," he said aloud, "You wanna provide, here's your chance."

Although Sunday morning services were over, El Santuario was crowded with summer visitors. He stood at the edge of the parking lot for a moment, wondering why he had come. Because of Gibbs, he answered himself with a pang of remorse. He figured that was reason enough. He decided not to try to enter the chapel yet. Perhaps tomorrow the crowd would be thinner.

He walked around to the rear of the church and eased his way down the steep embankment toward the river. Although at this distance he couldn't see the little stream that Linda said was there, he could hear it. At the bottom of the bank the ground leveled out. A copse of sheltering willow trees bordered the stream. It would be a good place to camp, he decided. Though it was hot during the day, nights in the high country were cool. He could sleep beneath the willows, wash in the stream, and use the tourist rest room just outside the church. That took care of everything, except his stomach.

He remembered that Linda had described a small store that advertised food just to the east of the footbridge near the church. He climbed back up the hill and saw that the little building in the southeast corner of the parking lot was fronted with a sign large enough for him to read:

SANDOVAL STORE

He could make out several people eating at a counter inside. Donning his binocular glasses, he scanned a menu that was posted on the porch near the door. Sweet rolls were twenty-five cents. He made a quick calculation. If he limited himself to one sweet roll a day, and drank only water, he could subsist for several days on the money he had. He put the glasses back in his backpack and decided to return that evening for "dinner."

Bone tired, it came to him that he hadn't slept for over thirty-six hours. Since learning about Gibbs, the day before, he'd been operating on adrenaline. He went back to the willow grove, unrolled his sleeping bag onto the ground and lay down atop it.

He awakened to the crimson glow of a setting sun, famished. Soon it would be too dark for him to find his way around in this strange place. He hurried back up the hill to SANDOVAL STORE, hoping that it was still open. It was. He entered, sat at the counter, but didn't pick up a menu.

"Can I help you?" a male voice said. The accent was distinctly Spanish.

"Sweet roll," George replied, without looking at the speaker. "And a glass of water."

Fifty-four-year-old Ruben Sandoval was a slightly-built man with a receding hairline and cherubic face. He had been born in Chimayo, and for the last thirty-one years had held a full-time job at nearby Los Alamos National Laboratory. He and his wife, Adelina, established the little store in anticipation of his upcoming retirement from his job.

Sandoval brought a pineapple-topped pastry and tumbler of water to the counter, then readjusted his tortoiseshell glasses and studied the young customer.

"You here for a cure?" he asked.

"Huh?"

"I saw you looking at the menu outside this afternoon... had some sort of spyglass on your head. I wondered if you're here for a cure."

Sure is inquisitive, George thought. "Nah... just curious." He took a huge bite out of the roll.

"No need to be embarrassed," Sandoval said. "I've seen more than one get pushed into El Santuario in a wheelchair and come out on their own two feet. You see all those crutches on the wall, inside the sacristy?"

"Yeah," George replied.

"When someone receives a blessing in El Santuario, they always leave a gift. That's tradition. Those crutches and wheelchairs say it all."

"Yeah, I guess so." George finished the roll, gulped down the water and stood. "How much I owe you?"

"Where you staying?" Sandoval asked.

"I got a sleeping bag down by the river." George pulled some change from his pocket and held it close to his eyes to count. "How much did you say?"

"Gets mighty wet down there when a rain comes up," Sandoval said. "This is the season for it. I got a small travel trailer parked out beside the store. My wife and I don't use it much anymore..."

George shook his head. "I don't have enough money for that."

"Who said anything about money? Go get your things. I'll unlock the trailer and leave the key inside on the table. Stay as long as you like."

George was at a loss for words. "I... I don't know what to say."

"No need to say anything. Get your stuff."

When George got back to the trailer, the icebox was stocked with milk, bread, cereal, cold cuts, juice, pickles, condiments, and a package of sweet rolls. The bed was made with fresh linen.

He sat down on the edge of the couch, incredulous at this unexpected benefaction from a complete stranger. At that moment the mocking prayer he'd uttered that morning resounded through his mind: *Okay, Lord... You wanna provide, here's your chance.*

"Oh, my God," he uttered aloud, beset with a jumble of conflicting emotions.

Years later, George would learn that he was not the first recipient of Ruben and Adelina Sandoval's benevolence. What they did for him that August, they had done for many needy pilgrims to Chimayo over the years. It was, in the words of one of the Sandovals' friends, "those good people's personal ministry in the work of the Lord."

George was too weary to contend with his conflicting feelings that night. He undressed and got into bed. He'd try to make sense out of it later.

For the next three days, more from curiosity than compulsion, he joined the worshipers who crowded into El Santuario from dawn to dusk.

On the first day, he sat on the front bench directly behind the large *candelabro*, where he could make out the dim visages of supplicants lighting candles and praying before the altar. Those who could, knelt. Many, unable to kneel, prayed from the confines of a wheelchair, or while others supported them, or while they supported themselves on crutches. Occasionally, a devotee would crawl the length of the aisle from the front door to the altar on his or her knees. Watching those who clasped a rood, or crossed themselves at prayer, George figured that fewer than half were Catholic. Somehow, that made him feel less of an intruder. Still, when he left the chapel that evening, one thought was uppermost in his mind. Every person he had seen approach the altar that day on crutches, left on crutches. Every person who had entered in a wheelchair, left in a wheelchair. If there had been any miracles at El Santuario that day, he had not witnessed them. It didn't occur to him until long after he'd gone to bed that night that once again he had entered and left El Santuario without uttering a single prayer.

On the second day, he was drawn toward El Posito, the pit of holy earth. For a long while he stayed in the sacristy, just outside the chamber that housed the pit, walking among the crutches and canes and wheelchairs that adorned the walls. From time to time he donned his binocular glasses and read a testimonial attached to one of the items. Finally, he ducked through the low door into the small chamber. He stood against the back wall watching pilgrims rub dirt from the sacred well onto various parts of their bodies. One man mixed dirt and water in a tumbler George recognized as coming from Mr. Sandoval's store and drank.

In this room, too, was the *bulto* of Our Lord of Esquipulas, the glass-enclosed crucifix where the elderly man had knelt in audible prayer the day that George first visited El Santuario. Suddenly, compelled by a force he didn't understand, he dropped to his knees on the earthen floor before the *bulto* and began to pray.

He prayed for the soul of his dear friend T. G. Gibbs, that he would reside forever in paradise with the Lord he so dearly loved. He prayed for his mother, in gratitude for her selfless devotion and for being his anchor to reality during that final suicide-prone year they had lived on Long Island. He prayed for his grandparents, for Aunt Linda, for Snow White, for Lois, for Piper, for his fellow students at NMSVH who were condemned, as he was, to live their lives less than whole persons. Abruptly, he turned to the sacred well, grabbed a handful of dirt and rubbed in onto his eyes. "Oh, God!" he cried out, in an impassioned plea. "If you're really there. Help me!"

Emotionally drained, he remained there on his knees until he regained the strength to rise. He made his way out of the chapel, went directly to the trailer and fell onto the bed.

When he awakened the next morning at dawn, he was still blind.

Utterly disillusioned, angry for having succumbed to emotion over reason, he gathered his equipment to return home. When he went to return the trailer key, the store had not yet opened for the day. Mouthing a curse of frustration, he retreated to a stone bench just outside the chapel courtyard to wait for Mr. Sandoval to show up. Within minutes it began to rain. Closer to the church than to the trailer, he entered the chapel and sat on a back bench. The darkness at the rear of the nave upset him and he moved forward to the front-row bench behind the *candelabro* where candles from early mass still flickered. After a moment, he felt compelled to look up at the large *bulto* of the crucified Lord. What happened next is paraphrased here in George's own words:

> "Suddenly, I was surrounded by a light so bright that it hurt my eyes, me, a blind man! Something made me turn around. When I did, I saw hundreds of people, men and women, on crutches, or in wheelchairs, or feeling their way along with white canes. They were struggling toward me, they had their arms stretched out to me, they were pleading with me! I wanted to scream at them, to tell them to go away, to leave me alone, that I was blind... and there was nothing I could do to help them. Then I was there among them. And I was running, not walking from one to the other, touching them. Then the crutches and the canes and the wheelchairs were gone. We were whole! And together we ran and ran and ran... toward the light...
>
> "Just as quick as it started, it was over.
>
> *"I realized then that I hadn't moved from that bench. And I was absolutely terrified."*

In that moment of awe and fear, George fled from the chapel to the courtyard, where he nearly collapsed. He made it to the stone bench, buried his head in his hands, and began to weep. His body was racked with sobs. He was still crying when he felt a hand on his shoulder. "Are you all right, son?" a familiar voice asked.

He looked up into the face of Ruben Sandoval. "I... I think I just had..."

He couldn't find the words.

Sandoval had witnessed such scenes before. "Take your time. I'll be in the store if you need me."

Much later that morning, George told Ruben Sandoval what had happened to him in El Santuario. "I was really scared," George revealed. "I didn't know what to make of it. Then, while I was sitting outside there on the bench trying to sort it out, it came to me. I've always thought of myself as a handicapped person. Well, I'm not. I'm a person *with a handicap*. I think that's what God was saying to me. I think he was telling me to quit dwelling on what I don't have and concentrate on what I do have. I've got bad eyes, sure, but there's nothing wrong with my heart or my lungs or my legs. I think that's what the vision meant."

Deeply moved, Sandoval said, "George, I, too, believe the Lord has spoken to you. But I'm afraid some people will scoff at what you've told me. You're going to have to be prepared for that."

George nodded agreement. "Nobody knows more about people scoffing at you than I do. Funny thing is, fellow I know... once knew, that is, tried to tell me that I could make a difference as a runner if I'd try. I wouldn't listen to him. He's responsible for me coming to Chimayo, though. Maybe it all ties in."

"Guess you'll be going home now. You've got to tell your family and all."

George hesitated. "Do you need the trailer back right now?"

"It's yours as long as you need it."

"I'd like to stay another night, then. There's one more thing I have to do."

Chapter
15

The "one more thing" George had to do was suggested by Ruben Sandoval the day they met. "When someone receives a blessing in El Santuario," the store owner had said, "they always leave a gift."

As he sat on the stone bench that third day following his vision, George worried about that. He had no wheelchair, no crutch, no cane to leave as a gift to express his heartfelt gratitude for the rich blessing he felt he had received. He would continue to need his binocular glasses in the future. The money he had was pathetically inadequate. As he wondered what he could do, he spotted a pile of lumber near a shed under construction in the picnic area. Rummaging through it, he found a piece of half-inch-thick particleboard about eighteen inches square. It gave him an idea.

Next morning he retrieved the board, took it down to the stream and washed it clean, then set it in a sunny spot to dry. In the arid desert air that took about ten minutes. He carried the dried board back to the bench where he put on his binocular glasses. Then, using a black felt-tip marker he carried in his backpack, he began to print on the board in large letters. Four hours later, composing with youthful enthusiasm, without revision, he had written:

I AM BLIND, TRAVELED MANY MILES TO CHIMAYO, A PLACE I LOVE. IN ITS SILENCE AND PEACE I LEFT THIS GIFT... A POEM.

IF YOU ARE A STRANGER, IF YOU ARE WEARY FROM THE STRUGGLES OF LIFE, WHETHER YOU HAVE A HANDICAP, WHETHER YOU HAVE A BROKEN HEART, FOLLOW THE LONG MOUNTAIN ROAD, FIND A HOME IN CHIMAYO. IT'S A SMALL SPANISH TOWN SETTLED MANY YEARS AGO BY PEOPLE WITH A FRIENDLY HAND, THEIR CULTURE STILL LIVES TODAY, THEY WILL TELL STORIES ABOUT MIRACLES IN THE LAND. SINCE 1813 SANTUARIO IS THE KEY TO ALL GOOD, A CHURCH BUILT AS GRACEFUL AS A FLOWER SWAYING IN THE SUMMER

BREEZE, NESTED IN A VALLEY PROTECTED BY WILD-
BERRY TREES.

IN THE DUSTY ROADS OF CHIMAYO LITTLE CHILDREN
WITH BROWN FACES SMILE, MAJESTIC MOUNTAIN TOPS
RULE OVER THE VIRGIN LAND, WHEN THE DAY IS DONE
THE SUN FALLS ASLEEP WITHOUT REGRET, SLEEPING IN
THE TWINKLE OF A STARRY SKY, STARRY NIGHT. IT'S
THAT OLD-COUNTRY FEELING IN CHIMAYO I CAN'T
FORGET, IN ALL THE PLACES IN THE WORLD I HAVE
BEEN, THIS MUST BE HEAVEN...

    G. MENDOZA

That noon Ruben Sandoval read George's gift twice
through without comment.

George said, "It's all I've got to give. I was going to leave
it by the door."

Ruben Sandoval shook his head. "No, you're not leaving
something like this by the door. You're going to present
this to Father Gonzales in person."

Reverend Father Francisco Gonzales was head pastor at El
Santuario de Chimayo. He and Ruben Sandoval had known
each other for years. Ten minutes after Sandoval called the
church office requesting an audience, the three men met in
the courtyard outside the chapel.

As Sandoval had done, Father Gonzales took a long time
to read through the poem.

George waited nervously. "I was going to leave it by the
door. But Mr. Sandoval thinks maybe you'd put it in the office.
Anywhere's okay. It's just something I wanted to say."

"Come with me," Father Gonzales said, in his heavy
Castilian accent.

He led them through the nave, past the sacristy, into the
chamber of El Posito. There, the priest placed the poem in a
stand-up position on a table against the wall opposite the
bulto of the crucified Christ.

"What a magnificent tribute to our Lord," he said.

Then, in that most sacred room in El Santuario, George
Mendoza dropped to his knees to receive Father Gonzales'
personal benediction.

In years to come, the poem George left with Father
Gonzales that day became one of the most venerated icons
in El Santuario. Supplicants prayed before it. Visitors copied
it, photographed it, memorized it. Church officials reprinted

it in brochures describing the chapel. Reproduced onto a postcard, it became, and remains, one of the best-selling items in El Santuario Gift Shop.

Ruben Sandoval arranged for a trucker to take George to Santa Fe that afternoon, where catching a ride south to Las Cruces would be easier. Before leaving, George entered El Santuario one more time to thank God for the miracle. When he came back out to the courtyard he told Sandoval, "I can't see any better than I could. But I'm no longer blind."

Sandoval walked with George to the parking lot to await his ride. "There's another tradition, you know."

"What?"

"It's customary to return to El Santuario every year in the month you first received a blessing."

"Then I'll be back every August," George vowed, "for as long as I'm able to come."

As the truck pulled into the lot, he grasped his benefactor by the shoulders and embraced him in a heartfelt hug. Then he left for the long trip back to Las Cruces and a new life.

The vision George Mendoza experienced in El Santuario de Chimayo has been the subject of widespread speculation among clergymen, media, and laymen.

In a letter referring to George's experience, Reverend Father Jose Maria Blanch, a pastor at El Santuario, stated it thus:

The church has never made any official investigations into miraculous cures. In the end, any result is ultimately due to one's own faith and hopefully, it may be God's will that whatever intention is desired, it will bring peace of mind and body. For many, (El Santuario) is a place where they can find solace from the world's pressures and demands.

In yet another insight into church position, Father Donald Starkey offers this commentary:

The burden of proof of a cure is on the claimant, not the church. When such is presented as a "cure," after medical evidence of some exceptional happening, then the church may or may not look to the claim. The church, in no way, stands or falls on such subjective happenings. Historical percentages do not favor such investigations.

Among George's acquaintances, there are those who believe that he merely suffered a hallucination brought on by the fatigue of three days of constant supplication. Others speculate that he had a nervous breakdown. Still others, skeptical of any account of spiritual intervention in the affairs of humans, dismiss the entire episode as fantasy.

In contrast, Ruben Sandoval, who was the only person to observe George closely during the days and hours directly preceding the incident and the first to see and speak with him afterward, is convinced that "the young man was touched by God."

To George, no further explanation is necessary. He is as unshakable in his conviction today as he was the moment it happened, that on that August day in 1974, in El Santuario de Chimayo, he was the beneficiary of a miracle.

Chapter
16

Within days after the fall semester began that year at New Mexico State University, teachers, students, friends, and family alike were talking about the "new" George Mendoza. No one was happier than Cindi. Overnight, the often-recalcitrant, habitually brooding son she had coped with since the onset of his illness had been transformed into a new person.

The first significant evidence of George's renewal came at school. He approached his teachers one by one and requested that they allow him to take oral exams rather than continue to struggle with laborious written papers. He explained the procedure that his history teacher, Robert Kelly, had instituted for him at Centereach High School on Long Island, and how it had helped him improve his grades. He agreed to find readers on his own, if that type of help became necessary. Every teacher concurred.

Next, he began to switch to subjects with a new goal in mind. In the past, he had remained in school primarily to please his mother. Now, instead of opting for the minimum, and easiest, courses required to complete a semester, he sought classes in psychology, sociology, and communicative skills. He explained to Cindi. "Someday I want to help people—people like me, who have a strike against them. I've been there, I know the score. I think I can get through to them."

First, he had to get their attention. And he'd already decided how to do that.

During their last meeting, that night beneath the cottonwood beside the San Juan River, Gibbs had said, "*You could make a difference for all of us… you could be a champion.*"

With his late friend's assessment of his potential as the catalyst, George began a demanding physical training program. Out of shape from months of inactivity, he began at a slow pace. Evenings, he performed calisthenics in his room. During sunlit hours, he ran around the block where he lived, where long before he had memorized every fence, every telephone pole, every shrub alongside or near the sidewalk. Afternoons after class, he pumped iron at the university gymnasium, often late into the night, to rebuild flabby muscles and develop a rhythmic breathing pattern. By the end of September, he decided he was in shape to undertake a more rigorous routine.

On weekends, he would pack his running clothes in a tote bag and hitchhike out of town. Sometimes he'd catch a ride to White Sands National Monument, near his old alma mater in Alamogordo. In this unique and exceptionally picturesque monument in the national parks service, where even he had to wear sunglasses as protection against the fierce solar reflection, he would run barefoot up and down the giant alabaster dunes, strengthening feet, knees, calves, and thighs. It was like working out in a desert of unblemished salt that extended for miles in all directions.

Other days he would call Philip Shapiro, his one-time track coach from NMSVH, and now a good friend. The two would drive to Stahmann Farms, the world's second largest pecan grove, ten miles south of Las Cruces. There, on 3,600 level acres, a series of arrow-straight rows, thirty feet wide, stretched endlessly between mature trees large enough for George to see. The rows formed perfect training paths. After measuring an exact mile, the two would run together, while Shapiro kept time with a stopwatch. By the end of October, George had cut his time from 4:44.05 to 4:36.10. A respectable time, but not nearly good enough.

In the fall, he began a cryptic routine which he played close to the chest. In the years immediately following the onset of his blindness, no longer able to depend on his eyes, he developed an almost encyclopedic memory for names, phone numbers, street addresses, even routes. On car trips, friends were amazed when he could tell them well in advance what intersection they were approaching, which way they should turn, how many miles remained in the trip. Now, he capitalized on that ability to further his running career.

That November, leaving his running clothes at home, he would hitch a ride to the foothills of the Organ Mountains, ten miles east of Las Cruces. At Dripping Springs road, he'd get out and walk three miles south to where a well-worn trail ascended the crest. For the rest of that day he would hike the trail, a distance of ten kilometers, memorizing every boulder, every cactus, every up and down and twist and turn of the terrain. Though he often talked with Cindi about the progress of his training at White Sands, and at Stahmann Farms, he never mentioned the trips to the Organ Mountains. For good reason.

One evening at dinner, shortly after Thanksgiving, she asked him, "Why didn't you take your running suit today?"

"I just went for a hike," he said, without looking up from his plate.

She knew he was not telling the truth. He'd always let her know where he went when he left town, just in case something happened, so she'd know where to look for him.

He must have sensed her doubt. After a moment, he said, "The Baylor's next month. I'm... going to try it again."

She stopped eating. It was a bad dream, recycled.

The previous December, quite unexpectedly, he had announced that he'd signed up to compete in a race he called "the Baylor."

"Just to see what happens," he said.

Cindi was surprised. He had quit running after graduating from NMSVH the previous June and hadn't even kept up his training. Still, she shrugged it off, assuming that he was going to be competing again with some of his visually handicapped friends from Alamogordo. She had no inkling that the Baylor was one of the most grueling cross-country races in the country—for runners with normal vision.

The following Saturday he returned home barely able to walk. He was covered with bruises and abrasions. There was a long cut over his left eye. He had fallen, he told her, as she cleaned his wounds. "No big deal." He didn't reveal to her that he'd failed to see one dogleg turn on the downhill course, had tumbled head over heels down a rocky embankment, and had clawed his way back up the bank to continue the race.

The following Monday, in her office, Cindi learned about the perilous race her son had competed in that weekend.

The Baylor Pass Run is recognized by serious runners as one of the most challenging in the sport. Designed in 1971 by a dedicated harrier who laid out the course to exact measurements using a topographical map, the race attracts top runners from throughout the Southwest. Beginning in the foothills of the Organ Mountains, the narrow trail ascends four precipitous miles up the west face of the mountain to a 6,000-foot crest (a 1,500-foot altitude gain), then descends

two zigzag miles down the east face to the finish line at
Aguirre Springs recreation area. Consisting of steep grades,
switchback turns, and sudden dips in terrain, the race is not
for the faint-hearted. There is scarcely a spot on the trail
wide enough for two persons to run side-by-side. Spotters
with radios are posted at intervals along the way. An official
on horseback follows the runners. Some runners,
unconditioned to the altitude, have collapsed. Others have
required first-aid on the trail, or had to be helped down by
horseback. All entrants must sign a disclaimer for injuries
before participating.

Thirty runners completed in the 3rd annual running of
the Baylor that December in 1973. The winner, Leon Garcia,
crossed the finish line in 40 minutes, 16 seconds. Twenty-
six minutes later, George Mendoza crossed the line—in 28th
place. He was bruised, bleeding, and disgusted with his
performance.

That night, as he limped to bed, he declared to Cindi,
"Don't worry. Never again!"

Now, a year after vowing that he'd never do it again, he
announced that he was going to re-enter the Baylor Pass
Run.

Trying to keep calm, Cindi said, "George, you promised.
It's just too dangerous."

"Not *dangerous*, Mom," he differed. "Rugged, sure. It takes
a 100 percent effort all the way. But outside of being in the
mountains, it's not a lot worse than other races I ran in at
the blind school."

She wasn't convinced. "Look what happened to you last
year. You fell off the trail. No, it's just too risky, I don't want
you to do it."

He reached over and put his hand on her's. "Mom, I
don't want to hurt you, but… I'm not asking for permission.
It's something I have to do, for reasons of my own. Besides,
it's not gonna be like last year. I've been over every inch of
the Baylor these last few days. I know it now like the back
of my hand. Don't worry, okay?"

She realized that to object further would risk spoiling the
new rapport they had established in the past few glorious
weeks since he returned from Chimayo. She gave his hand a
squeeze. "All right. I won't bother you about it again. But I
will worry."

Thirty-six official runners entered the Baylor that blustery

Saturday afternoon in December 1974. There were three unofficial entries (runners not desiring official recognition of their time). One was George Mendoza.

On the first mile, George set the pace. With his peripheral vision glued to the edge of the track, he went gung ho to establish as much distance as possible between himself and the pack. At the end of the first mile, where the trail involves steeper switchback turns, he slowed his pace. For the second and third miles, sticking to the outer brink of the course, he maintained his position among the front runners. Then, midway through the fourth mile, with the crest almost attained, he began to fall back. His legs were on fire, In the chill, rarefied air, his breathing was labored. By the time he reached the top, he was faltering near the rear of the pack. On the downward course he fell into last position, and remained there for the remainder of the race.

Sixteen-year-old Darlene Taylor, a first-time entrant, finished last in the official category that day with a time of 1:20.16. George crossed the finish line a full minute later— fifteen minutes longer than his time the year before.

During that previous attempt at the Baylor, George had been dispirited with his performance. This time he wasn't. For now he knew what was wrong—his training. Many runners could "race the clock" in training. They extended as much effort running against time as they did against an opponent. George was not one of those runners. Recalling his dismal best for the mile at Stahmann farms that summer—4:36.10—he realized that he would never be a clock runner. When he was setting records for NMSVH two years before, he had not raced time, he had raced the man ahead of him. He had done the same in training with the NMSVH track team. Now, his self-developed training routine at White Sands and at Stahmann Farms had helped him rebuild weakened muscles. But it hadn't restored his once-vaunted endurance and speed. He needed to train against competition. Not just any competition—with runners who put forth their best at all times and would push him to do the same.

The following Monday at the university, George went to the arena where the New Mexico Aggie track team was practicing under the watchful eye of Coach Art Morgan. Morgan, a medium-sized man with prematurely silver hair, had inaugurated the school track team in 1965. His athletes had systematically broken records in the Big West Conference (formerly the Pacific Coast Athletic Association). The coach held a special affection for the Baylor Pass Run and would later take over hosting it. He spotted George on the sidelines.

"How'd you do Saturday?" Morgan called back to him.

"Ran out of steam," George replied. "I want to talk to you about it."

"Oh?" Morgan came to where George was standing.

"Coach, I'd like to run with the Aggies."

Morgan was taken aback. From the silence, George knew that he'd given the wrong impression. "I mean," he added quickly, "that I'd like to *train* with the Aggies."

"I see. How come?"

"I want to compete again," he replied, "if I can get my act together." He explained his doubts about his self-developed training methods. "I need real competition. Running against a stopwatch just isn't gonna cut it for me."

Morgan understood. He knew all about runners who did well racing the clock, and those who didn't. "Sure," he agreed. "You know our schedule. Just don't expect these guys to cut you any slack."

George was delighted. Soon he would be training with one of the finest track teams in the Southwest.

But first, there was another matter he felt he must resolve before he could get on with his life. Something that had obsessed him for years. Quite by chance, that morning before going to see Coach Morgan, he had overheard a conversation in the student union building that brought the issue to a head.

Chapter
17

The conversation George had overheard that morning took place while he was taking a coffee break in the Student Union after his first class. He had just finished and was getting up to leave when he heard three students at a nearby table talking about jobs they had gotten as extras in a movie being filmed near Las Cruces. It was a common experience for college students in New Mexico. One of the talkers mentioned being in a scene with Slim Pickens.

George sat back down and turned toward their table. Excusing himself for eavesdropping, he asked, "Did you say Slim Pickens is in the movie?"

"Yeah," one of the trio confirmed. "Him and one of the Mitchum boys. They're shooting an oater. They can probably use you if you want to sign up."

"Where's it being shot?" George asked.

"Radium Springs."

That afternoon when he got home George asked Cindi, "Mom, who's that Hollywood actor you said knows my dad?"

"Slim Pickens. Why?"

"Just wondering."

Next day, George skipped afternoon classes and hitchhiked to Radium Springs.

The lonesome desert country around Radium Springs, New Mexico, eighteen miles north of Las Cruces, had been favored by movie makers ever since Paramount filmed *Redskin* in the area in 1928. When George arrived on the set that day, the action was well under way. As on most movie sets, guards were posted to provide security for the actors and staff. George got as far as the catering trailer before a security guard stopped him and asked to see his pass.

George explained that he had no pass. "I just wanted to talk with Mr. Pickens."

"Not much chance of that," the guard said, gruffly. "If you want to stick around, you'll have to get a pass. That trailer over there."

George could see that the man was pointing. "I'm sorry... I can't see that far."

"Can't see?"

The guard put his face closer to George's. After a moment, his tone friendlier, he said. "I'll go see what I can do. What's your name, young fellow?"

"George Mendoza... Junior."

"Take a seat in one of those canvas chairs there; they won't be needing them for awhile. I'll go see what I can do."

Ten minutes later the guard returned. "Slim's gonna be tied up for the rest of the day. He says if you'll drop by his hotel tonight, he'll be glad to talk with you. He's at the Sagebrush in Las Cruces."

Delighted with the news, George thanked the helpful guard and left.

That evening, George had his Aunt Linda drop him off at the Sagebrush Inn. She told him to give her a call when he was ready to go home and she'd come get him.

Slim Pickens greeted George warmly at the door of his suite. "Danged if I knew there was a George Junior. Come on in. Let's get acquainted. How 'bout a Coke or maybe a glass of tea? Don't have nothing stronger."

"Coke, please" George said.

He was captivated by the graciousness of his host. The veteran cowboy actor whose commonplace features were recognizable by millions of movie fans around the world was as affable in person as he was on the screen. George felt at ease.

Pickens fixed a couple of Cokes on ice at the wet bar and brought one to George.

"You see many cowboy movies, son?" he asked. Almost at once, he apologized. "Hey, I'm sorry, buddy. Guess that was a stupid question, considering what the security guard told me today."

"That's okay. I don't go to movies. I watch TV sometimes. Up close I can make out some of the action. Are those boots real lizard skin?"

Pickens laughed and lifted his leg. "Now they're loud enough for anybody to see, ain't they? Yep, real lizard. Hold on a minute."

He went to another room and came back with more boots and laid them out in the light in front of George.

"These here are alligator, these over here are ostrich. Even got some sealskin ones around here somewhere... or did I bring 'em?"

Pickens showed George other paraphernalia he wore on the current movie set, and in other films he'd made. "Wore this hat in Dr. Strangelove..."

"Hey!" George interjected. "When you rode that H-bomb down outta the belly of a B52. I saw that one when I could still go to movies. That was fantastic!"

"Well, thank you, partner. That was sorta wild, wasn't it?"

They chatted for a while about movies in general, and the stars Pickens had worked with over the years. Finally, Pickens sat back in his chair and asked, "Now, what was that you wanted to talk to me about, son?"

Before coming, George had wondered how he was going to ask the questions he wanted to ask. Now, encouraged by Pickens' good nature, he said, "Mister Pickens, how come you know my dad?"

"Oh? Well, we used to do a bit of fishing together. Fine man, your dad. How come you ask?"

"Do you have any idea where he lives?"

Pickens was taken aback. "You mean, you don't?"

"No, sir."

"That's what this is all about then? You want me to tell you where your dad lives?"

"Yes, sir."

Pickens was obviously leery. "I'm afraid I don't understand what's going on here, son."

He told Pickens how his mother and father had separated when he was still a baby. How he had no recollection of his father, other than a couple of short visits when he was a youngster.

"I see," Pickens said. "Now, just what would you do if I did tell you where your dad lives?"

"I don't know. Go see him, I guess. I'd just like to get to know him, learn more about who I am."

After a moment, Pickens got a piece of hotel stationary from the desk. "Your dad lives in New York." He wrote an address on the paper handed it to George. "Hope I'm doing the right thing, for both of you. Good luck, son."

George shook hands with his amiable host, thanked him, and left.

As soon as he got home that evening he showed the address to Cindi.

"Are you going to write to him?" she asked.

George shook his head. "J. R.'s going to New York over the Christmas holidays. I'm going to ask him if I can ride along."

For years, Cindi had dreaded that someday this moment would come. She wondered how she would react. Now, though troubled, she kept her misgivings to herself.

"You'll need some extra money," she said. "I'll cash a check tomorrow."

The day after Christmas, George and J. R. Gomolak, a fellow student at the university, left for New York.

A week later, bored with an empty house, Cindi decided it was time to make a trip she'd wanted to make since summer. She wanted to see for herself the little chapel where her son had come to grips with his life. Early one morning, she left for Chimayo.

Beautiful any season of the year, in winter the village of Chimayo is breathtaking. On this day, the high country north of Albuquerque was blanketed in white. The snow-covered hills, roadways, and trees reminded Cindi of scenes from her childhood in New England—except for the houses. The rambling adobe homes, with their angular architecture and rich earth tones, were uniquely Southwestern. A heady aroma of burning piñon wafted from their chimneys. It was the type of scene, she imagined, that first captivated the renowned artists who had established internationally famed art colonies in nearby Santa Fe and Taos.

In the midst of this enchanting setting, El Santuario de Chimayo shone like the jewel in the crown that it was. The uncrowded parking lot signaled that there were few visitors here on this winter day. She parked near the wooden bridge and hurried past the icy courtyard into the little chapel. She stood in the rear of the nave until her eyes adjusted to the subdued lighting, then moved slowly along the aisle, taking in all the marvelous paintings, icons, and *bultos* George and Linda had described to her. At the altar, she stood for a long while looking up at the carved likeness of Christ on the cross, into the symbolic eyes that had beckoned her son to a vision that had changed his life. She uttered a prayer of thanksgiving, then moved into the sacristy that housed the wheelchairs, the crutches, and the canes that told silent stories of other supplicants who had received blessings here.

She stepped into the El Posito chamber and immediately spotted what she most wanted to see. On the east wall, prominently displayed now in a special niche, rather than resting atop a table with other offerings, was George's poem, the gift from his heart that he had left at El Santuario, because he had nothing else to give. She read the poem through several times, comprehending in the heartfelt words the transformation of spirit that others could never discern. Deeply moved, she took her pen from her purse and wrote in the border near George's name: *I love you, Mother.* Then, with a final prayer, she left.

(Eighteen months later, Cindi again visited El Santuario alone. On this occasion she joined a tour group being conducted through the chapel by a priest. When they reached the El Posito chamber, she was surprised to see that George's poem had been scrubbed clean and encased in Plexiglas.

"It used to hang in its natural state, just as Mr. Mendoza wrote it," the priest explained in relating the story of the poem. "Then some unthinking person scribbled on it. After that, everybody started signing it, or leaving messages around the border, even between the lines. It became almost unreadable. A kind person restored it for us, and, as you can see, it's protected now. It's difficult to understand people who would defile such a valued treasure."

Cindi joined the others who clucked their tongues and nodded in disgust. It would be years before she would confess that she was the "unthinking person" who first "defiled" her son's gift to El Santuario)

Following her first visit to El Santuario, Cindi arrived home in mid-afternoon. When she entered the house she spotted George's suitcase in the hallway.

"George," she called, eager to talk about New York.

He came out of his room carrying his sleeping bag and camping gear. "I have to go to the mountain for a couple of days."

"But you just got home," she protested.

"I was going to leave you a note. I just need to be alone for awhile, to think things through."

"Did you... see your father?"

"Yeah." He didn't expand.

"And?" she prompted.

"And, he's got his life, and it's time that I got on with mine."

He gave her a cursory buzz on the cheek. "Don't worry. I'll be back soon."

With a heavy heart, she settled into a chair and watched him leave. She knew now that her misgivings about his trip had been warranted. She said a silent prayer that whatever had occurred would not cause her son more pain than he'd already suffered.

It was a prophetic concern.

Chapter
18

Early in 1975, George reported for spring training with the New Mexico Aggie track team. He would continue to train with them for four years. Later in life, reflecting on those years, he would credit his association with the Aggies as the turning point in his athletic career.

Just as Coach Morgan had predicted, the Aggies gave no quarter on the training field. Though they greeted George warmly, and several of them became his good friends, the prevailing view was that he was more than just another runner to beat in their quest for favored team status. He was a threat. To be beaten by a blind man, even in practice, would have been intolerable. It was an attitude to George's liking. It pushed him to the limit of his abilities, and he learned tricks he could not have learned elsewhere.

To develop speed, he trained mostly in the 440, 880, and 1,500 meter events. Unable to see the turns in the oval track, or even the width of the track, he stuck to his accomplished routine of keeping his peripheral vision fixed to the edge of the course as he ran. That method had worked well in competition with other blind runners, who understood their opponents' handicap and often allowed for it. Unlike them, the Aggies didn't give a second thought to flailing elbows, kicking feet, and sudden changes in position. More than once George found himself jostled from the track by an unwitting (in most cases) runner.

To compensate, he began to concentrate on another physical sense. More than once, while running on a mountain trail, his superb sense of hearing had detected an angry rattlesnake in time for him to jump aside. Now, by fine-tuning this ability, he learned to discern by sound the position of other runners, how many were behind or ahead, whether they were gaining on him or falling back. Eventually, combining the physical senses of acute hearing and limited sight, he began to cross the finish line ahead of some of the Aggies.

It made him cocky. If he could beat some of the best

varsity runners at the school, he concluded, he could beat them all. One afternoon, as he approached the final turn in the 880 event, he threw caution to the wind. Ignoring the edge of the track, he moved toward the center, raised his head, and went into a furious win-or-die kick toward the finish line. Seconds later he overran the track, sped across the end zone, and crashed full force into the bleachers. The next thing he knew, he was lying flat on his back and someone was holding a wet towel to his aching head.

"What the hell were you trying to do, Mendoza?" a voice asked.

George made out the blurred face of an assistant coach hovering above him. With the coach's help, he managed to get to his feet. "I stumbled," he said meekly, struggling to keep his balance. "You got any aspirin?"

It was his last attempt to defeat all the New Mexico Aggies.

One day after practice, Coach Morgan called him aside. "Your speed's fine," Morgan told him. "But you're jumping the gun, If you want to be competitive in the big leagues, you've got to have endurance."

Thereafter, whenever the Aggies went on cross-country runs, George went too. In addition, he began his own cross-country routine. On weekends, and often on weekdays after school, he'd hitch a ride to the high mesa east of Las Cruces where he had worked for the Bureau of Land Management. There, where his coworker Carlos had warned him to be wary of rattlers, he would run for hours along the ancient cattle trails, rebuilding the breathing pattern he had enjoyed at NMSVH. He figured that if he could endure in the rarefied air at this altitude, he could endure anywhere.

It was also with the Aggies that George learned the diet he would follow for the remainder of his competitive career. The day before a race, his evening meal would consist of two or three copious servings of pasta. In keeping with this, Cindi kept her cupboard stocked with spaghetti and macaroni. On the day of a race, he ate only toast and tea laced with honey before competing. It was a regimen favored by many athletes, and when George traveled to competitive meets, he would always find those foods on the menu.

In January 1975, an event occurred that eventually would play right into George Mendoza's plans to make a mark in the world on behalf of the handicapped. The International Sports Organization for the Disabled (ISOD) announced that the blind would be invited to compete in future Olympiads for the Physically Disabled, beginning with the games scheduled for the following year in Toronto, Canada. It was a long overdue concession.

The Olympiad for the Physically Disabled was held every four years in the same year as the regular Olympic games. Inexplicably, since its inception in 1952 at Stoke Mandeville, England, to encourage athletic activity among victims of paralysis, the Olympiad had excluded blind athletes. Officials could not conceive of a blind person running, jumping, or performing other Olympic-quality feats that were performed routinely by men and women with other impairments. It was a preconception that would soon be shattered.

Seventeen hundred athletes representing fifty countries competed in the 1976 Olympiad for the Physically Disabled in Toronto. Twenty-seven blind athletes represented the United States—twelve track and field (including swimmers), ten wrestlers, and five distance runners. In all, these dedicated young men and women garnered nine medals, three of them gold. The gold medal winner for the 100 meter event, establishing a record-breaking time of 11.4, was George's one-time NMSVH classmate, Winford Haynes.

Haynes, who was born blind, grew up in Alamogordo, New Mexico. Wrestling and swimming were his favorite sports as a youth. Then, at the New Mexico School for the Visually Handicapped, he tapped a remarkable ability for track. By the time of his win in Toronto, he was regarded as the fastest blind runner alive. He returned to Las Cruces a local hero.

Enthralled by Haynes' accomplishment, George went to congratulate him. During this meeting, Haynes told George about a new organization being formed to represent American blind athletes.

"USABA," Haynes said.

"You-sah-bah?" George repeated phonetically.

"United States Association of Blind Athletes. Why don't you sign up? If you keep improving, you might even qualify for the next Olympiad."

George was hesitant. "You think I'm good enough?"

"I think you could be. Look... I can't even see the finish line, but I know it's there. You just give it all you got and go for what you know is there."

That November, the United States Association of Blind

Athletes was created to foster competition in swimming, track and field, gymnastics, wrestling, Alpine and Nordic skiing, goal ball, and power lifting. Headquartered in Beach Haven Park, New Jersey, USABA consisted of twelve regions throughout the United States. Prompted by Winford Haynes, George Mendoza became a charter member of Region 8, comprising New Mexico, Texas, and Oklahoma. Committee representative for the new region was Jack Harmon, one of George's coaches from NMSVH.

Four months later, along with his fellow athletes from Region 8, George traveled with Coach Harmon to Western Illinois University in Macomb to participate in USABA's first annual national championship competition for the blind. One hundred eighty men and women from twenty-two states vied for medals that March and April of 1977. Running in national competition for the first time, George competed in the 1,500-meter event.

At the sound of the gun on that blustery spring day, George sprinted ahead, bent on putting as much distance as possible between himself and the other runners. Before he finished the first lap, he realized his error. Instead of pacing himself at the start, to get a feel for the competition, he had tried to win the race in the opening seconds. Trying to compensate, he slowed his pace, hoping to reserve energy for the final lap. By the end of the third lap, the other racers had passed him by. On the final lap, with 180 meters to go, he went into his final kick. One by one, he overtook the competition, except for a single runner he could hear but not see. Judging from the sound of the leader's feet striking the track, George estimated him to be about four meters ahead. He tried to increase his kick, but the energy he had expended in his initial sprint from the starting line had taken its toll. He crossed the finish line in second place, without ever gaining the final few feet on the winner. His time was a disheartening 5:00.0.

That evening in bed, unable to sleep, he replayed the race over and over in his mind. Angry at himself, he realized that he had repeated the mistake Coach Morgan had warned him about. He had jumped the gun, just like he'd done during his first attempt at the Baylor three years before. He had tried to win the race in the first few seconds. He hadn't won the Baylor, he hadn't won today, and, unless he learned to pace himself, he would never win a race in the future.

The future.

He remembered something Winford Haynes had said to him during their trip to Macomb. They had been talking about the 1980 Summer International Olympic games scheduled to be held in Moscow. The Olympiad for the Disabled was always held in the same year but not necessarily the same country as the regular Olympic games. Haynes mentioned that plans were underway for the disabled athletes to hold their meet in Holland.

"If you make a good showing in Macomb," Haynes had said, "and keep it up in the nationals for the next couple of meets, you just might a win berth on the USABA Olympic team."

The Olympics!

To George, the mere thought of competing in Holland was intoxicating. Just to be accepted as a member of the team would be an honor. But to win would be...

Suddenly, the recollection of his performance today broke off that heady thought.

He would never qualify for the Olympic team by repeating that day's performance. To have any chance in Holland—of even being invited to Holland—he would have to win at the nationals. And he'd have to win *big*.

He knew the problem. You don't win races by being first out of the starting gate. You win by being first across the finish line.

He threw back the sheet and sat up on the side of the bed, engrossed in thoughts of what he must do. Two national competitions remained before selections were made for the 1980 Olympiad team. He had two years left during which he must prove himself or forfeit the dream.

Chapter
19

As he had done every summer since 1974, that August George made his annual pilgrimage to El Santuario de Chimayo. During these visits he would sit on the same front-row wooden bench just behind the *candelabro* where he had experienced the vision that had changed his life. There he would offer thanksgiving for the gift he had received and ask for guidance in days to come.

Nowadays, instead of remaining in the village overnight, he usually planned the sojourns for a single day, departing Las Cruces at first light and hitchhiking back that evening. Still, he never journeyed to Chimayo without paying a visit to his old friend, Ruben Sandoval.

On that first morning following devotions, he went to Sandoval's store, where the proprietor greeted him warmly and dished up one of the pineapple sweet rolls he always had on hand when George dropped by. While eating, George told Sandoval about the upcoming Olympic games for the disabled to be held in Holland. Then he lamented his performance at the USABA national meet in Macomb. "There're a couple of more national meets before they pick the Olympic team," he said. "If I can't win in the nationals, I've got about as much chance of going to Holland as I've got of becoming an airline pilot."

"Is Holland that important to you?"

"You bet it is. How am I ever gonna be able to convince someone who's blind, or maybe in a wheelchair, to put up with the pain it takes to go for the gold if I can't get there myself?"

"Not everybody's good enough to win a gold medal, son."

"I know that. But making the effort's one hell of a lot better than sitting around being miserable. That's all I want them to do. Just try. Win, lose, or draw... just *try*. But first, I've got to get their attention. It's winners people listen to, not an also-ran."

"You still running with the Aggies?"

"Every day."

Ruben nodded toward the little chapel across the courtyard. "Did you ask *Him* about the Olympics?"

"All morning long," George replied, pensively.

"Then you'll be okay," Sandoval predicted.

That fall, the beginning of his final year at New Mexico State, George once again called on his old friend Phil Shapiro for help. Shapiro agreed without reservation.

For the next six months, in addition to running with the Aggies, George and his one-time NMSVH coach undertook a new approach to training. Each weekend they drove to the western foothills of the Organ Mountains.

There, on the broad open mesa, they would stake out a 1,500-meter oval track. Then, the two would run together. A few inches shorter than George, but just as trim, Shapiro set a steady, energy-reserving pace for the first couple of laps. Unaccustomed to holding back, George would sometimes break pace and try to rush ahead. At such times, Shapiro would grab him and yank him back into position.

"It was like training a dog to heel," George would explain later, with a reminiscent laugh, when relating the story.

Somewhere during the final lap, at Shapiro's signal, the two would increase stride. By now, George had developed the prancing high kick that would become a trademark of his style. Side by side, they would charge the finish line at a furious do-or-die pace.

On other days, Shapiro would run behind George, or ahead of him, or far to the side, challenging George to detect from sound where the coach might be. In nearly every case, George was able to pinpoint Shapiro's position within a couple of feet.

Early in 1978, USABA announced that the national meets scheduled for that spring would once again be held in Macomb, Illinois. On the basis of his second place showing in the 1,500 meter race the year before, George was once again selected to represent the blind for District 8.

A couple of weeks before the New Mexico team was scheduled to leave for Macomb, George hitchhiked alone to the mesa. He reset the 1,500-meter markers Shapiro had put in place for a full mile. Then, simultaneously triggering a stopwatch, he pushed off from the starting line. Four minutes, seventeen seconds later, he crossed the finish line— his personal best.

The unofficial time of 4:17.00 that George set that day on the mesa would never enter the record books. Nonetheless, he was overjoyed. In months of grueling retraining since he returned from his first trip to Macomb, he had learned to pace himself to preserve his endurance and had increased his speed. He realized that no matter how much he worked at it in the future, he would never be better than he was on this eve of his second departure for the nationals. The moment of truth had come.

On a bright Friday in March, on the playing fields at Western Illinois University in Macomb, George Mendoza crossed the finish line in the 800-meter race a full four paces ahead of his nearest competitor. His time, 2:16.00, was less than one second from the national record set the year before.

On the bus ride home that weekend, joyous and feeling vindicated, George Mendoza wore the gold medal of a winner around his neck the entire trip.

Chapter
20

In the fall of 1978, George graduated from New Mexico State University with a bachelors degree in individualized studies, including major credits in counseling services.

In the audience that day was Felix Serna, a prominent New Mexico artist and photographer, and local businessman, who attended the ceremony for the sole purpose of seeing George receive his diploma. Serna had met George soon after he moved to Las Cruces. During George's glory days on the track at NMSVH, Serna had become deeply impressed with the blind boy's pluck and determination. In time, the two became great friends, and Serna became one of George's ardent fans and promoters. He and George had talked many times about George's ambition to become an advisor to the handicapped after graduation.

Following congratulations that day, Serna handed George a brochure. "You might be interested in this."

George couldn't make out the small print. "What is it?"

"It's about a program to help kids. They may not be handicapped physically, but they've got their problems. Take a look at it with your reading machine."

That afternoon in his room at home, with the aid of his Visualtek, George studied the brochure. It described a counseling program designed to help wayward and needy children between the ages of ten and eighteen. Known as CHINS (Children In Need of Supervision), the service was funded by the federal government under the Comprehensive Employment Training Act. Impressed by what he read, the next day George applied for a job with the organization. Following a brief interview, he was selected for the position of counselor.

His job with CHINS was as rewarding to him as it was to the young people he counseled. On call day or night, he worked with youths who were struggling to cope with stressful situations in and out of their homes. Some were dropouts from school, some habitually disobeyed parents and other authorities, some were runaways, some were suicide-prone. Whatever the symptom, George recognized the underlying affliction common to all—low self-esteem. In dealing with them, he had two factors in his favor: he had been there himself, and he was something of a local celebrity.

After he returned home from Macomb that spring with the gold medal of a winning runner, the local media learned that the blind boy who had set varsity records at NMSVH was still around. His feat at the USABA national meet was chronicled on the sports pages. Some of the stories included his photograph. In his new job, his medal and the newspaper clippings of his accomplishments on the playing fields became valuable counseling tools. Whenever he was assigned to the case of a recalcitrant boy or girl who was suspicious of authority figures—as were most of the youths at CHINS—he would bring out the medal and the clippings.

Like most youth, the kids in the CHINS program were fascinated by sports heroes. Their reaction to his simple trappings established the rapport George needed to proceed to the next stage of his strategy. Having gained their confidence and their attention, he told them the story of a young athlete who lived on Long Island in New York, and who with his pick of college scholarships, suddenly went blind. He led them through the somber days of the boy's life, describing how he suffered derision from fellow students, how he was hurt by confrontations with insensitive coaches, how the lack of understanding from teachers drove him from school. He told about the boy's thwarted suicide plans, his bitter clashes with his mother, how he was crushed by the death of his closest friend. Then, having described the darkness, he brought the kids back into the light. He told how one day in a quiet little chapel, the boy gained a new perspective on life. Because of federal restrictions, he couldn't emphasize the religious aspects of the story. Nonetheless, he explained how the insight the boy gained in the chapel that day caused him to come to grips with his true affliction. "It wasn't the blindness of his eyes that was crippling him. It was the blindness of his spirit, and it caused him to give up."

By this time in the recitation, most of the children had guessed the boy's identity. "It was you, huh?"

"Yes, it was me," he would confirm. "I realized then that there was no sin in failing. The sin is in not trying."

He would pause to let the lesson soak in. Then he'd bring

the story full circle by describing how he had returned to running, to school, and to life. Picking up the gold medal, he would hold it out for them to observe and say, "And this is only the first one. I'm going to try for more. Will you help me try?"

Thereafter, it wasn't unusual to see George Mendoza running along a street or a parking lot in Las Cruces paced by a young boy or girl who acted as his eyes. It was one of the most innovative approaches to counseling in the history of CHINS.

In addition to his full-time job at CHINS, George continued his demanding training regimen on the oval track at NMSU with the Aggies and on the mesa or among the pecan groves at Stahmann Farms with his running guru, Phil Shapiro. The routine they had established the year before had proved successful at Macomb. Now, the sessions were geared toward preserving that routine.

The prudence of that strategy was soon put to the test.

In March 1979, George accompanied the Region 8 team to the USABA national meet in Seattle, Washington. In a race jammed with contestants, he took the 1,500-meter event with a time of 4:31.7—a new USABA national record. In literature describing the meet, USABA proclaimed George Mendoza "a rising star."

The final qualifying meet before USABA selected athletes to represent the United States in the Olympiad for the Disabled in Holland was held in Macomb in March 1980. Going for a double win, the "rising star" won the gold in the 800-meter race with a time of 2:12.79. The following day, in a punishing race paced by an aggressive front-runner who led all the way until George finally overtook him on the final turn of the third lap. George crossed the finish line in the 1,500-meter event with a time of 4:28.00.

Although disabled-athlete meets attracted few fans, those who were there that day roared their approval of the cliff-hanging spectacle. As a USABA official placed the gold medal around his neck, the loudspeakers blared with the announcement that George Mendoza of New Mexico had just established a new world record!

The small crowd went wild.

Felix Serna was the first to greet George when he returned from Macomb. "Nothing can keep you from going to Holland now," Serna enthused, grasping George's hand. "Nothing!"

Beaming his delight, George agreed.

In the spirit of triumph, neither of them could foresee the ominous cloud that would soon descend over George, and his fellow athletes, disabled or not, throughout the nation.

Chapter
21

In a whirlwind twenty-four month period George had picked up four gold medals, established three national records, and one world record. He was no longer merely a local story. Print and broadcast journalists from Albuquerque, Santa Fe, El Paso, San Antonio, Los Angeles, St. Louis, Phoenix, New York, Atlanta, and many other cities phoned for interviews with the blind runner from Las Cruces. It was the opportunity George had dreamed of since Chimayo. Though willing to share his triumphs with the world, he demanded that the full story be told, warts and all. He regarded this extended coverage of his feats as another opportunity to reach out to the disabled, to inspire them through his own story to strive to overcome.

In April, USABA announced the names of fifty disabled athletes who had qualified in the nationals to represent the United States in the Olympiad for the Disabled that summer in Holland. Three New Mexicans were on the list: Winford Haynes, Clifton Randolph, and George Mendoza.

To mark the occasion, on May 27 Governor Bruce King summoned the trio to Santa Fe. In a laudatory ceremony in his office, the governor proclaimed "Blind Athletes Week" throughout the state and honored the three runners by presenting them certificates of appreciation printed in Braille. A reporter in the room asked George to "read" the certificate aloud for the press. George was stumped. He didn't have the slightest idea how to read Braille. Sensing the predicament, another reporter intervened with a question about the Olympiad which changed the subject. That afternoon, on the car trip back to Las Cruces, Winford Haynes "read" George's certificate to him.

Selection for the International Olympiad was the opportunity George had been seeking. If anything could bring him the stature he needed to transform his dreams to reality, an Olympic gold medal would do it. Cindi, too, was excited by the confirmation that her son was going to Europe—for a reason that transcended sports. The year before, learning that the Olympiad for the Disabled would be held in Arnhem, Holland, Cindi experienced a renewed surge of hope. She knew that the Netherlands shared a common border with Belgium. Researching her atlas she found that Arnhem was approximately 125 miles from Gent, where Dr. J. Francois, the ophthalmologist with whom she had corresponded years before about George's affliction, had his office. In Arnhem, her son would be just a short train ride from the world's leading authority on fundus flavimaculatus!

On the day USABA announced that George had made the list, Cindi phoned Dr. Francois' office. Through his receptionist, she arranged for the doctor to examine George at 2:15 p.m., Wednesday June 25—two days after George was scheduled to run in the 1,500-meter race in the Olympiad. That evening she impressed upon George the importance of keeping the appointment. "He's the leading authority on your disease. Whatever happens at the Games, seeing him is every bit as important."

George agreed. "I'll keep the appointment, Mom."

Shortly thereafter, an event that had occurred four months earlier darkened hopes that George would ever see Holland or Dr. Francois.

On December 27, 1979, the military forces of the Soviet Union invaded Afghanistan. Condemnation of the attack was universal. Ignoring the public outcry, the Soviet hierarchy pressed ahead with their attempt to gain a strategic overland route to the major oil fields in the Middle East.

President Jimmy Carter, confident until then that he had established a workable rapport with General Secretary Leonid Brezhnev, considered the invasion a personal affront. In concert with other world leaders, he called on the Soviets to halt the aggression. To add teeth to the American position, he declared a ban on cooperation with the Soviet Union until Soviet troops were withdrawn from Afghanistan. Included was a boycott of the upcoming Olympic Games.

The Olympic community was stunned. For many young athletes, the Moscow games were a once-in-a-lifetime opportunity. Now, their dreams were shattered.

At first, neither the International Sports Organization for the Disabled (ISOD) nor USABA saw reason for concern. There was no official connection between the International Olympic Games to be held in the USSR and the Olympiad for the Physically Disabled to be held in Holland. The ban applied to Moscow, not Arnhem. Plans for the Olympiad for the Disabled continued without interruption.

Then reality set in.

As was true for the regular Olympics, the Olympiad for the Disabled received no government funds. Operating costs were underwritten by corporate sponsors and financial offerings from the public. Following the president's ban, donations ceased, not only for the regular Olympics but for the Olympiad for the Disabled as well.

Alarmed, USABA directed local regions to publicize that the presidential ban did not apply to the Olympiad for the Disabled. Still, the coffers remained bare.

At the end of March, concluding that only President Carter could altar the public's misconception, the St. Louis Society for the Blind forwarded an appeal directly to the White House:

March 31, 1980
Mr. Jimmy Carter
President of the United States
The White House
1600 Pennsylvania Avenue
Washington, D. C. 20500

Dear Mr. President:

Due to public confusion over your recent pronouncements regarding the 1980 Summer Olympic Games in Moscow, we feel that we are being unduly hampered in our attempts to raise the necessary funds to send our blind athletes to *The Olympiad for the Physically Disabled*, which will be held in Arnhem, Holland, June 19th through July 6th, 1980.

Therefore, we are urgently requesting you to demonstrate your obvious compassion for the handicapped by seeing to it that a public statement is made to the effect that these Olympic Games have nothing to do with those being held in Moscow, and that you ask for public and private financial support for our efforts.

On March 25–29 the United States Association for Blind Athletes National Championships were held in Macomb, Illinois. At these competitions 50 young athletes were selected to join the more than 200 physically disabled individuals who will represent the United States in Holland this summer; each of them must raise at least $2,000.00 for the trip.

Mr. President, we respect your efforts to make the position of the American people most clear with respect to their nation's response to the unwarranted and unacceptable Soviet aggression in Afghanistan and around the world. However, we ask for your support in allowing our Olympic program for blind athletes to go forward, unimpeded by this unfortunate confusion.

As April 15, 1980 represents a deadline for collection of the needed funds, we humbly urge your speedy response to our request for assistance.

We thank you so much for your cooperation in this matter, and we remain

Most Sincerely,

The letter was signed by Tom Culliton, President, Missouri Chapter for the United States Association of Blind Athletes; the Reverend Neal J. Carrigan, St. Louis Society for the Blind; and David P. Wicks, St. Louis Society for the Blind.

Across the country, athletes scheduled to go to Holland waited for the definitive statement they were confident President Carter would make to the press on their behalf. But the deadline came and passed without response.

In mid-May, hoping to nudge the White House to act, the St. Louis Society for the Blind released a copy of their letter to the media. United Press International (UPI) transmitted it via their wire service to newspapers nationwide. Editorial response was almost universally favorable to the cause of the disabled athletes. As a follow-up, UPI queried the White House as to why no response had been forthcoming. The White House press secretary replied that no such letter had been received. The secretary hadn't reckoned with the fact that the St. Louis Society for the Blind had certified the letter and requested a return receipt. Confronted with the receipt, the White House responded in a letter addressed to Father Carrigan:

Dear Father Carrigan:

Thank you and those who joined with you for your

message to President Carter. He is pleased that you took the time to tell him about your organization, and we regret that the volume of mail on hand prevented an earlier reply.

I must explain that, as much as the President would like to support all of the worthwhile projects brought to his attention, it is not possible for him to do so. He receives so many special requests that he believes it would be unfair to assist a few groups while excluding others which may be equally deserving. I hope you will understand.

The letter was signed by Daniel M. Chew, director of presidential correspondence.

Despite the President's refusal to help—perhaps because of it—the publicity UPI gave the interchange of letters was the catalyst the situation needed. Throughout the country, celebrities, local businesses, and individual citizens rallied to meet the financial needs of the disabled athletes chosen to go to Holland. St. Louis Cardinals offensive lineman Terry Stieve offered two tickets to any Big Red game in 1980 to any person making a donation of at least $75 to the Missouri Chapter, USABA. Spearheaded by Stieve, the St. Louis drive netted $6,000.

Similar appeals played out across the country. In Las Cruces, Felix Serna and Cindi, with the generous aid and support of award-winning New Mexico playwright Mark Medoff, set about to raise funds for the three state sons chosen to represent their country in the Olympiad. Restaurants, fast food outlets, and other businesses catering to the public collected funds in prominently displayed *Send our boys to the Olympiad* containers. Churches, fire and police department auxiliaries held bake sales and garage sales. Private citizens posted themselves in parking lots, supermarkets, and other strategic locations to solicit funds.

In June, as a result of this community outpouring, the three New Mexican Olympiad athletes left for Holland. As she drove George to the airport, Cindi reminded him again of his appointment with Dr. Francois.

"I won't forget, Mom. Don't worry."

She wished him luck with a kiss, then watched him board the plane for the first leg of the journey. She hoped the best for him at the games in Arnhem.

But her prayers were focused on Gent.

rge Mendoza, age 17, on his graduation from the
 Mexico School for the Visually Handicapped
SVH), Alamogordo, New Mexico. *Credit: NSMVH*

George, age 14, a few months
before the onset of the illness.

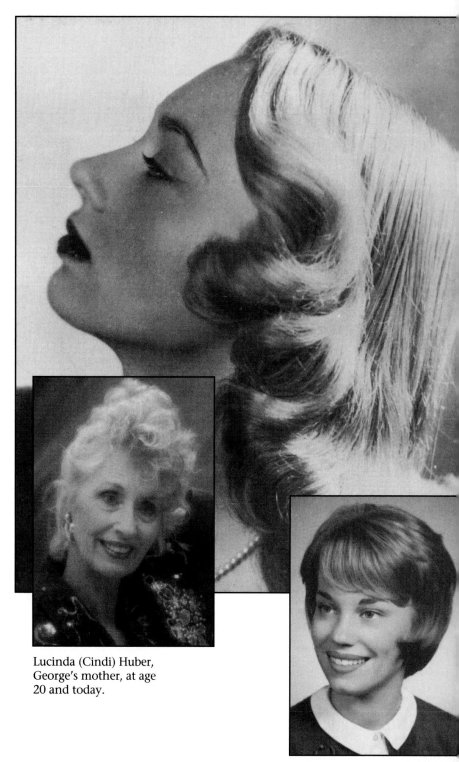

Lucinda (Cindi) Huber,
George's mother, at age
20 and today.

Linda Huber, George's aunt.

VH wrestling team, George's senior year. George is #9 (cleanshaven for wrestling), ford Haynes is #2, T. G. Gibbs is to the far left, and coach Jack Harmon is to the far . *Credit: NMSVH*

cation Hall at the New Mexico School for the Visually Handicapped.
it: NMSVH

(Inset) George and Linda near the barren mesa where George asked her to take him to El Santuario de Chimayo (above), "the Lourdes of America." *Credit: Felix Cordova Serna*

The entrance to the courtyard at El Santuario de Chimayo. *Credit: Felix Cordova Serna*

El Posito, the sacred well where the Holy Cross was found. Here George fell to his knees and prayed for deliverance from his affliction.
Credit: Felix Cordova Serna

George's offertory poem on the piece of particleboard he wrote it on, in its privileged place in the El Posito chamber.
Credit: Felix Cordova Serna

George's sympathetic benefactor, Ruben Sandoval, seated before his store near El Santuario de Chimayo. He was the first to witness the change in George following the "miracle." *Credit: Evelyn Jacque*

George's running coach from NMSVH and personal friend, Phil Shapiro.

George training on the New Mexico State University track for the 1980 Olympics in Holland. By fixing his limited vision askance to the white line on the outer edge of the track, he could maintain his position. *Credit: NMSU*

George and his mother on the day of his graduation from New Mexico State University. *Credit: Linda Huber*

George's wife,
Maria.

George's daughter, Guadalupe.

George's son, Michael.

Chapter
22

June 1980.

Two thousand men and women representing forty-four countries gathered in Arnhem, Holland, that summer to compete in the Sixth International Olympiad for the Physically Handicapped. Over the next two weeks, fifty Americans, thirty-four men and sixteen women, would vie with other world-class athletes for the gold, silver, and bronze in twenty separate events, including track and field, weight lifting, wrestling, archery, cycling, wheelchair soccer, table tennis, equestrian skills, fencing, and others.

At the opening ceremony on Saturday, June 21, track co-captains George Mendoza and Winford Haynes stood enraptured as fellow athletes with normal sight described the pageantry, the multitude of flags, the colorful flower-bordered playing fields, the magnificent stadium filled with thousands of enthusiastic spectators. The pointed contrast between the ardor displayed by European fans for these handicapped games and the near-apathy such events evoked in the United States seared the memory of every American athlete there that day. It was a comparison George would never forget, and one that would have a significant impact on his future.

As was true throughout the International Sports Organization for the Disabled, the visually handicapped were assigned to compete against others in the same class. The classes were ranked A, B, C, in decreasing severity, with Class A representing the totally blind.

Class A entrants raced while lightly holding onto a bar or string stretched alongside the track as a guide. In most cases, both in practice and in actual contests, sighted persons were stationed at intervals along the track, and at the finish line, in case a runner overran the edge of the track or failed to stop at the tape.

With some exceptions, Class B and C runners were permitted to depend on their remaining sight, and sense of sound. The exceptions were during a long-distance race in a rugged area, or in any race where an official deemed added precautions necessary. In those cases, a sighted runner would run alongside the visually impaired runners to warn of obstacles.

During his first years in USABA, George had competed in Class C. The previous year, because of an increased loss of vision, he was re-categorized into Class B. Qualifying tests conducted in Holland prior to the games confirmed the new category.

The 1,500-meter Class B race was scheduled to be held on Monday, June 23. At breakfast the day before, Winford Haynes, who later would capture the silver in the 100 meter race, remarked to George that the word on the playing field was that the 1,500-meter race would be held in four separate heats.

"What do you mean? I haven't heard anything about that."

"Four different races, four groups of runners."

George was perplexed. He'd never raced that way before. Moreover, he and Haynes were co-captains of the American track team. Why hadn't he been briefed about the procedure by an official rather than having to hear about it in passing from Haynes? He pushed his breakfast aside and went to the field, where he cornered the first Olympiad official he spotted. Why, he asked, had the race been restructured, and what did it mean?

"There're too many runners for a single race," the official explained. "Too much chance for injury."

"You mean the winner of every heat will get a gold?"

"No. The winners of the heats will race each other for the medals."

"When? Tomorrow, after the heats?"

"Then, or perhaps later. It hasn't been settled. Either way, it's the fairest system we could come up with."

Maybe so, George thought, as he went to the dressing room to suit up for a practice run. But it also meant that the qualifiers would be racing twice, maybe on the same day.

That night he couldn't sleep. Around midnight, he got out of his cot, threw on his sweat suit and made his way down the well-lit halls to the rear entryway. He went outside and sat on a step with his back to the wall. Though he couldn't see it, he knew he was facing the playing field where he would race in just a few hours. His stomach was filled with butterflies. That's the way it was, sometimes, the night before a big event. He thought of the last time and smiled at the memory.

It had happened the night before he was to depart Las Cruces for Holland. After tossing fitfully for hours, he rose sometime before dawn, dressed, and went outside. The street in front of his house was bordered by two towering street lights spaced several hundred feet apart. Though he couldn't see any of the street between the lights, he could make out the area directly beneath either light when standing under it. To burn off nervous energy that night, he began to run from one light to the other, up and down the street whose features he had memorized years earlier. He'd been running about ten minutes when all of a sudden the piercing wail of a siren disrupted the night calm. He detected a flashing red light approaching and stopped in his tracks. Next, he was caught in the glare of a spotlight.

A car screeched to a halt nearby. "Police officers!" a gruff voice barked. "Put you hands on top of your head! Don't move!"

"Wha... what?" George exclaimed, dumbfounded.

"*Now*, fellow!"

George grabbed his head. "What the hell's going on? I didn't do anything?"

The commotion woke up the neighborhood. Porch lights switched on, people came out into the street. Then, George heard a welcome voice. "What on earth is wrong, officer?" Cindi asked.

"Robbery, Miss. Bowling Alley down the block. We caught this guy running away."

"Mom, I wasn't running away. I was just uptight about tomorrow. I couldn't sleep, that's all."

"Mom?" one of the officers said.

"He's my son," Cindi replied. "He lives here with me. He's nervous about leaving for Holland tomorrow."

"Holland?" The officer stepped closer to George. "Well, I'll be damned. George Mendoza. Why didn't you say it was you? Hey, Sarge... this is one of those guys that's been in the papers. He going to the Olympics."

"Can I take my hands down now?" George asked.

"Sure. Sorry kid. You better get inside with your mom. Lots of cops out tonight. Next one might not read the sports pages."

Somehow, recalling that raucous night at home eased his jitters. He returned to his cot and slept well until reveille.

Over the weekend, a low-pressure front had moved in from the North Sea, pushing cold, wet weather before it. Monday dawned to a darkened sky that threatened to burst into a downpour at any time. The list of participants in the 1,500-meter Class B race had been posted the evening before. George was to run in the second heat.

The first heat in the 1,500-meter Class B event was held shortly after 1:00 p.m. in a drizzling rain. In a splendid performance of championship running, Paul English of Canada broke the tape with a time of 4:21.00, seven seconds better than the world-record time George had set in Macomb three months earlier. Listening to the announcer describe the race, George realized that English was the man to beat. He thought back to the day on the mesa above Las Cruces when he ran a full mile in 4:17.00. He realized he would have to perform that well in the four-man race-off that day, or whenever, to win the gold. But first, he had to win his own heat.

At the starting gun for the second heat, George fixed his eyes on the outside stripe and pushed off at a leisurely pace, sizing up the competition on a wet track. By the end of the first lap, with little effort, he had passed most of the runners. He could hear two runners ahead. Half-way through the second lap, they came into his range of vision. He knew he could catch and pass them at will. He decided to hold back, to reserve as much energy as possible for the four-man race to come. On the final turn, he went into his final high kick, exerting just enough effort to pass the two front-runners. He won the heat in 4:26.00, two seconds faster than his world-record time.

He was barely winded. He realized that the unofficial time he'd set that day on the mesa above Las Cruces had been in rarefied air at six thousand feet. Here in Holland, in the oxygen-laden air at sea level, he knew he could do better. Eager to take on Paul English, and the winners of the other heats, he retreated to the athlete's lounge to rest.

That's where he was, lying on his back on a rub-down table, when Winford Haynes brought him alarming news. "There's not gonna be any more heats."

George sat straight up. "What!?" Then, figuring it was a gag, he laughed. "Yeah, sure. C'mon, man, don't do that to me."

"Not kidding, George. They just announced it. Our guys are protesting it right now."

George realized his friend was serious. He jumped off the table and ran to the field. Coaches and runners from several countries were confronting Olympiad officials. There was a heated argument in process. The officials turned and walked away just as George pushed himself into the group. "What the hell's going on?"

"One of the guys slipped off the track in the last heat," one of the Americans answered. "The officials say it's too dangerous, track's too wet. They're awarding the medals to the fastest times already logged."

"No! No way!" George protested. "That's not what was agreed. Hell, man, I wasn't pushing for time in my heat. I'm supposed to get a crack at those guys."

"They won't bend, George. They claim now that there never was any intention of holding a four-man race-off. I'm afraid we've been had."

The fastest three times already logged belonged to Canadian Paul English and his two runners-up in the first heat. They were awarded the gold, silver, and bronze. George's time, although two seconds better than his world record, was fourth.

Incredulous, George went looking for the American team leader. Unable to find him, he returned to his dormitory and changed to his street clothes. He had converted half of his $400 expense money into guilders on arrival at the airport. He stuffed the local currency into his pocket and left the Olympic village in a rage.

It was a flagrant violation of Olympiad rules. Before departing for Holland, George and his fellow athletes had signed a code of conduct regarding absence from the village (prior permission was required) and a strict curfew. At this moment, he didn't give a damn about the code of conduct or curfew.

Blinded now by fury as well as affliction, he stalked the streets of Arnhem, bumping into strangers and stumbling over curbs. Incurring the wrath of horn-blasting motorists, he crossed streets with reckless abandon. At one intersection he turned onto a narrow side street and collided with a large stand-up, A-frame sign placed in the center of the sidewalk. Printed in oversize letters at the top of the sign was the one English word found in most every country in the world: BAR.

He located a door beside the sign, entered, and made his way to a wooden booth in the rear. Moments later a hefty waitress came to the table. She said something he didn't understand.

All he could think to say was, "Heineken?"

"Ah. American?" the woman said. "You touring?" The words were heavy with accent, but she was speaking English!

"Yes." He pulled out the wad of guilders and tossed it on the table. "Could you bring me a beer?"

"Bottle? Pitcher?"

What the hell, he thought. "Pitcher."

Three pitchers later, George stood and looked around desperately for the men's room. Wobbly on his feet, he grasped the back of the booth to steady himself. He couldn't make out anything in the darkened bar.

The waitress approached. "You are all right?"

"I can't see. I have to go to the bathroom."

She moved closer and stared into his face. "Your eyes are a problem?"

"Yes. Bad problem."

"Ah." Her tone expressed regret. She led him down a hallway to the men's room, took him up to the urinal, and stood there. "I will wait."

He had been briefed that continental Europeans didn't suffer the puritanical hang-ups of Americans. The need to relieve himself was urgent. But he wasn't about to pee in front of a strange woman. *If* he could help it. "No. That's okay. I can find my way back."

She must have sensed his discomfort. "Yes... all right. You call if need me." She left.

He had memorized the way and found his way back to the booth with no problem. He sat down and poured the last dregs of beer from the pitcher and drank it in a gulp. Then he leaned back against the wall. Within minutes, he was sound asleep.

He was awakened by the waitress tugging at his arm. "It is our time to close," she said.

"Close? What time is it?"

"It is after midnight."

Oh, my God, he thought. Not only had he violated rules by leaving the Olympic village unescorted, he was in violation of curfew. Despite the spinning in his head he was sober enough to realize that he was in trouble. He also realized that he could never find his way back in the darkness.

"Could you get me a cab?" he asked.

"Cab?"

"A taxi cab. To the Olympic village."

"Ah, taxi. You wait."

She returned with a man she introduced as a taxi driver. Then, picking up the guilders which George had left on the table since arriving, she paid the cab fare in advance, then stuffed the rest of the money into George's shirt pocket.

"He will take you," she said.

He thanked her for her kindness and let the taxi driver help him to the car.

At the Olympic village, the security guard who checked his pass asked if he had been drinking. George figured his breath had already answered the question. "Yeah," he said.

The guard made a notation in his ledger and ordered him to report to his team leader the next morning.

That Tuesday, an ad hoc committee of USABA team leaders was appointed to consider disciplinary action against George. One member was his friend and co-captain, Winford Haynes. With no formal meeting room assigned for such purposes, the members of the committee who assembled (some would not attend) met on the steps of the dormitory.

Nauseous with a hangover, George listened dispassionately while the committee debated a proper punishment. A majority felt that he should be confined to the village for the duration of the games. Haynes, who knew of George's promise to his mother to keep the medical appointment in Belgium, and knew that he *would* keep it, come hell or high water, made the point that this was George's first violation of USABA rules in the years he'd known him, and suggested a mild censure. The majority disagreed, arguing that the number of infractions—leaving the village unescorted by a sighted person, inebriation, violation of curfew—were too serious for a slap on the wrist.

After additional debate, the majority voting for stiffer chastisement prevailed. The penalty was announced: restriction to the confines of the Olympic village.

"No way," George declared, "I won't accept restriction."

He considered making an appeal based on what Haynes already knew; that it was imperative for him to keep an appointment in Belgium. Then, remembering the rule against a blind athlete traveling without a sighted person with him, he realized that the upcoming trip would simply be another infraction. The only explanation he offered was: "It's a personal matter."

Despite committee pleas, George remained adamant.

Concluding that there was no recourse, the committee confiscated George's pass, ordered him to turn in his uniform, and expelled him from the team and from the village. They reminded him of the date and time the team was scheduled to depart for the States. If he was at the airport on time, he could return with them. Otherwise, he was on his own.

George shrugged at the punishment. Still rankled over what had happened at the games yesterday, he didn't care one way or another.

He went to his room and threw his belongings into his bag. Ninety minutes later he was on the train heading south to Belgium.

Chapter
23

The next afternoon, in his office in Gent, Belgium, Dr. J. Francois performed the most extensive eye examination George had undergone since the onset of his disease. It didn't take the famed authority long to reach a conclusion. When he finished, the doctor motioned for George to wait in the receptionist's office while he dictated his findings to a secretary.

George doesn't recall any exchange of conversation between himself and the doctor that day, but he does remember that the receptionist spoke perfect English. When he took a chair near her desk, he noticed a timeworn folder bearing in large print the name: GEORGE HUBER.

The records had to be his. "Looks like an old file," he remarked.

"It is quite old," the receptionist said.

"I didn't know you had records on me."

"We have records from other doctors that your mother sent to Dr. Francois." The file also contained copies of all the letters his mother and Dr. Francois had exchanged over the years.

Somewhat later, the doctor's secretary brought the receptionist a report not yet typed. The receptionist asked George if he would like to wait until she transcribed it into English so he could read it. "We have a visual aid machine."

George declined. "Would you read it to me, please?"

"Surely."

She read the document through once in silence, then translated it for him:

Mister George Huber presents on both eyes a juvenile macular dystrophy of Stargardt's type, associated with a fundus flavimaculatus. There is no treatment, but one can expect that if the central vision is lost, the peripheral visual field will be conserved.

She put the document down and glanced up at him. "I

am sorry it is not more encouraging. Do you wish a copy to take with you?"

It was precisely the diagnosis Dr. Rosen had made in Manhattan ten years before. "Could you mail it to my mother... in about ten days? That will give me time to talk to her about it before she gets it."

The receptionist made a note on her calendar. "Yes, I can do that."

He paid the bill from his expense money and left.

He was in no hurry to get back to the youth hostel where he'd spent his first night in Gent. He recalled that the taxi driver who picked him up that morning had mentioned passing a large park just before they reached the doctor's office. It had to be nearby. He began to walk. He had gone about a block when the sidewalk became shaded from what he could tell were swaying tree branches. He knew he had found the park.

Just inside the entrance he came upon an empty wrought-iron bench beneath a large tree. He sat down to ruminate about Dr. Francois' findings. He hadn't expected an upbeat diagnosis, so he wasn't too disappointed. Indeed, he was surprised to find that he felt a sense of relief. Now, perhaps, his mother would accept the reality he had come to accept long before. He wondered if he should call her. He decided against it. He wanted to be there when she learned this last and final verdict.

His thoughts turned to the events at the Olympiad that had brought him to this lowest point in his athletic career. Since yesterday, he had gotten his anger under control. But the bitterness remained and would remain, he knew, for a long time to come. He felt he had been cheated. He had never raced against the clock; he had always run to beat the man ahead. That's what he had done in his heat at the Olympiad, without even trying hard. And he'd won. Then, the opportunity to go for the gold had been snatched away from him.

Suddenly, he was engulfed by a sense of failure. He had failed his country and his teammates. He had failed Felix Serna, and Phil Shapiro, and Art Morgan, and the New Mexico Aggies, and all the others who had helped him train or had given so much of their time to raise the funds that made it possible for him to compete in the Olympiad. Most of all, he had failed himself. He had failed to achieve the capstone to his career, failed to ignite the beacon he once dreamed of holding high to rally others to better themselves, as he believed he was called to do that fateful day six years before at Chimayo.

At the thought of the little chapel, now so far away, he experienced an overwhelming feeling of homesickness. Just then, from somewhere in the deepest recesses of the brain where memories are stored, he heard a familiar slow-drawl voice from the past: "They ain't drowning in terminal self-pity... like you are."

Like you are.

He gave a nervous laugh. "Gibbs, you slippery rascal," he uttered aloud. "You won't even let me off the hook when you're dead."

Well, was it true? Was he lapsing yet again into self-pity? Time to get off that kick.

He forced his thoughts away from himself to the past few days in Holland. To the valiant displays of spirit of his fellow athletes. To the thousands of cheering people who crowded into Arnhem Stadium each day to witness ordinary people doing extraordinary things. It was the incessant topic of conversation among the American team—in the locker rooms, on the sidelines while waiting to perform, during meals, at night in the dormitory after lights out. They spoke of how wonderful it was to be appreciated, to be lauded by fans, to be recognized as world-class athletes.

What a glaring contrast it was, he mused. This genuine enthusiasm of European fans for the disabled athletes, compared to the relative apathy about them in the States. In America, the regular Olympics received hundreds of hours of media coverage, winners became heroes to the masses, overnight stars. Conversely, games for the disabled received little recognition—no winner ever became a star.

He thought back to his personal accomplishment over the past two years—four gold medals, three national records, one world record. Still, no national network came knocking at his door, no product sought his endorsement, no cereal manufacturer contracted to put his likeness on a box of flakes.

What could be done? he wondered. Would a dedicated spokesman who knew the pain be able to bring the story of handicapped athletes to widespread public attention? Could the reporters, the networks, the filmmakers be persuaded to recount the accomplishments of disabled athletes with the same regard they gave the non-disabled?

He felt a rush of adrenalin. It would be an exciting challenge... a challenge he would like to undertake.

Then, excitement was tempered by reality.

Notwithstanding Gibbs' lingering censure, there was no self-pity in facing facts. The fact was, he was no longer a winner.

And people would not be swayed by a loser.

Chapter
24

As was his custom, when he arrived in Chimayo that August for his annual pilgrimage, two months after returning from Holland, he went first to Ruben Sandoval's store. The little cafe was closed, the sign was gone. George donned his binocular glasses and tried to see through the window. The inside of the store was dark. He was standing there, with his face pressed to the pane, when a voice from behind asked, "Are you looking for something?"

He turned to see a young man in priestly garb staring at him. At the sight of the binocular glasses, the priest asked, "Oh, are you Mr. Mendoza?" The accent was heavily Spanish.

"Yes."

The priest stepped up on the porch and offered his hand. "I'm Father Miguel... or rather, now that I'm in America, Father Michael. Ruben told me much about you. He said you would probably come looking for him. I promised to watch for you."

George slipped off the glasses and shook hands. "What happened to Ruben. He's not sick, or... something?"

From the tone in George's voice, the priest could tell that the boy was quite found of Ruben. "Oh, no. He and his wife decided to sell and move where's it's warmer in the winter. He left his address for you. It's in the church office. Come."

As usual, El Santuario was crowded with summer visitors. George decided to wait outside on the stone bench. Father Michael went to the chapel, then returned and handed a piece of paper to George. "Ruben said to congratulate you for him. He said you would be wearing a gold medal."

George shoved the address in his pocket and gave a mirthless chuckle. "Well, I'm afraid I've disappointed him."

"Oh?" Father Michael studied George. "You seem troubled. Is there something I could do to help?"

George started to say no. Instead, he found himself telling the entire story to this young priest he had just met—the thrill of being chosen for the Olympics, the excitement of Holland, then how it all fell apart with the unfair race, the drunken spree, and his ostracism from the team. He even described his visit to Dr. Francois.

It had poured out from George in a torrent of words that revealed deep torment. When he finished, Father Michael asked, "How did you get back to America?"

"With the team. They wouldn't let me wear the uniform, but they let me fly back with them."

"I am sorry the eye examination was not more optimistic. I know Ruben will be also."

"I expected that," George said. "What I didn't expect was to come home a failure."

The priest objected to that self-assessment. "You have had a disappointing setback, I agree. But from what Ruben has told me about you, I certainly would not call you a failure. Not from this one venture. Neither would he."

They priest paused. They watched the tourists mill around outside the chapel for a moment, then Father Michael said, "Ruben has told me about the great solace you find in El Santuario—as we pray all who visit will. Have you been to the chapel yet?"

"Not yet. I was hoping the crowd would thin out some. I have a special place I like to sit." He rose. "I guess I better go on in, though."

Father Michael stood. "I will be in my office if you need me."

George thanked the priest for listening to his story, then left to enter El Santuario.

He was grateful to find that his favorite front-row bench was empty. Taking a seat near the large *candelabro*, he confessed in prayer that he had failed the task God had assigned him. Then, in a heartfelt plea, he asked for guidance in his life to come.

When he returned home from the pilgrimage that weekend, he packed his running clothes and shoes in a cardboard box and stored them on a top shelf in his closet. Some weeks later while cleaning, Cindi noticed the clothes were missing from where she always hung them after laundering them. She asked George what had happened to them.

He told her what he'd done. "I don't need them now. I guess I'll keep them as mementos of what was—and what could have been."

For Cindi, it was one more heartbreak in what had turned

out to be a joyless summer. She understood George's dejection over what had happened at the Olympiad. She'd even forced herself to come to terms, as George had done, with Dr. Francois' confirming diagnosis. But this additional act of withdrawal, coming on the heels of those other setbacks, set off alarm bells in her head. She feared that her son was once again on the brink of the black hole of depression that had shadowed his young life far too long. She made a silent vow to do whatever was within her power to keep that from happening.

One morning in December, Ernie Barge, one of George's former fellow students at NMSU, called to invite George to accompany him to a wedding that day at the parish church in San Miguel, a village south of Stahmann Farms. He mentioned the names of the bride and groom.

George knew and liked the couple, but a wedding would be another of those large church affairs where he would be able to see four or five rows ahead and nothing beyond. "I don't think so, Ernie. Thanks anyway."

"Come on, *amigo*," Ernie insisted. "I don't want to go alone."

George begged off.

Cindi had heard the call from the kitchen. "Who was that?" she asked, stepping into the living room.

He told her about the invitation.

She knew how he felt about large gatherings. But turning down opportunities to get out of the house had become all too routine for him lately.

"Ernie's been such a good friend," she pointed out. "Maybe you should go with him."

She was right about Ernie Barge being a good friend, George thought. Although born in the states, Ernie had lived in Brazil most of his young life. An accomplished linguist, he spoke fluent Spanish, a talent that came in handy during the many trips he and George took through remote New Mexico villages where English was regarded as a foreign language. More than once, Ernie had to explain to a villager why someone named Mendoza couldn't converse in the "native" tongue.

Ernie was also an accomplished musician. Often at college, when sleep wouldn't come, George would call Ernie and the two of them would take their guitars to the bleachers behind the school and play until dawn. Sometimes other students would join them for an all-night songfest. Other nights, Ernie would drive George to the desert where the two would study the sky and philosophize about life until time to report back to school for classes. On reflection, George could not remember a time when Ernie had turned him down. He felt a pang of guilt.

He called Ernie back. "Changed my mind," he said. "I'll be ready in an hour."

The old stone church in San Miguel occupied the site of one of the earliest Spanish mission churches erected in the lower Rio Grande Valley. A parish legend held that only good things happened there.

The church was filled that afternoon with friends of the bride and groom. As he'd feared, George found himself seated in a rear pew, where everything taking place at the altar was a dull blur. He had just settled back to make the best of a bad situation when he spotted a slender young woman sitting alone in the pew directly in front of him, her pretty face framed by ebony hair.

As he stared at the girl, he recalled something that had happened in Centereach before he went blind. He was shopping at a supermarket with his mother. As they turned one aisle, they passed a pretty young brunette pushing a cart in the opposite direction. Following her with his eyes, George emitted a low wolf whistle.

"George!" Cindi exclaimed.

"C'mon, Mom... she's a *dish*."

"She is definitely *not* a dish," Cindi reproached him. "Besides, looks are only skin deep. There're much more important qualities you should be thinking of when it comes to girls."

Uh-huh, he'd thought cynically, at the old cliché. No matter what mama said, one thing was for sure. Whatever qualities he sought in girls, looks were going to be high on the list.

Now he shifted slightly in the seat, focused his vision on "the dish" in the next pew, and looked at her throughout the ceremony.

The mild December climate in the valley permitted the wedding couple to hold the reception on the lawn. As the guests moved outside, George made a succession of frenzied maneuvers to keep the pretty brunette in sight. Once, as she made her way around a garden of native shrubs, he cut across, stumbled over an agave plant and almost lost his footing. When he regained his bearing, she was nowhere to be seen. Moments later, as he was looking around on all sides, she emerged from the midst of a cluster of people she'd been chatting with and walked right up to where he was standing.

"George Mendoza, if you intend to keep staring at me like this, you should at least know my name." She put out her hand. "I'm Maria."

Flustered, he reached for her hand, missed it, then finally grasped it. "How did you know my name?"

"I read the sports pages. Stay put. I'll be right back."

"Promise?"

"Promise," she said, and walked away.

She returned with two glasses of punch. She handed him one. "Take my arm," she directed.

She led him through the mingling crowd to a bench in the shelter of a large mulberry tree. There, she told him what she knew about him. He was astounded that she was able to quote the milestones of his track career, from his earliest days at NMSVH to his Olympiad race in Holland.

"How do you know all that?" he asked, bursting with pride.

"I'm a runner, too. Not a pro, but I enjoy it." Then she tempered his pride by quoting the records of USABA's Winford Haynes, Olympian Bruce Jenner, UNM Lobo John Baker, and other track luminaries.

"Okay. You seem to know a lot about me. Now, let's hear about you."

He learned that her full name was Maria del Rosario Escobedo. She had entered New Mexico at age nine with her parents, becoming a U.S. citizen before graduating from high school. She went on to New Mexico State University to earn a bachelor of science degree in elementary education, with a minor in bilingual education, and a master's degree in guidance and counseling. After college, she worked as an instructor of adult basic education and as a typist/translator transcribing English language tapes into Spanish for the foreign language department at NMSU.

"Now I'm a teacher at San Miguel Elementary School and am working on my doctorate."

"Good grief," George exclaimed. "No wonder you know how to read!"

Soon after the bride and groom made their rice-showered departure that afternoon, the guests began to leave the party. Maria saw Ernie Barge making his way toward them. "I think your friend's ready to go," she said.

George spoke hastily, "Look, Maria, this has been great. I can't remember when I've had as much... listen, I'd like to see you again, but... well, I don't drive."

"I do."

"Yeah... well, I don't have a car... or even access to one."

"I do," she repeated.

"Oh? Here?"

"Right here."

"Say, would you give a guy a ride home?"

"Sure."

He made his apologies to Ernie Barge, then rode home with Maria Escobedo. It was the beginning of a beautiful relationship.

In coming weeks, the sight of Maria's mint-new white Ford Mustang parked in front of the Mendoza home was a familiar one to residents on Baldwin Street. Sometimes they would stay there, where Cindi, delighted with the burgeoning courtship, would retreat to her bedroom, leaving the kitchen and living room to her son and his girlfriend. Maria remarked about that one day. "Your mother is a very special person."

"Bedrock," he said. "I haven't been the easiest person to live with. But I couldn't have made it without her." Then, with emotion bordering on anger, he added, "She's the only parent I ever had."

He took a special delight in introducing Maria to his friends. One day he asked her to drive him to Felix Serna's art supply shop. "He's a great guy. You two gotta get to know each other."

"We'll have to stop on the way for gas," she said.

It was a pump-your-own station with a sign reading: PAY CASHIER FIRST. She rummaged through her purse for her credit card. He jumped out and grabbed the hose. "I'll pump while you pay."

"Big deal," she quipped, but smiled to let him know it was in jest.

He was screwing the cap back on when she returned to the car. A half-mile from the station, the car began to smoke. By the time they pulled up in front of Serna's store, it looked as if the engine was on fire.

Felix spotted them coming while they were a block away. After they pulled up to the curb, George and Maria piled out coughing and fanning fumes. Felix grabbed a fire extinguisher and ran out to raise the hood, but the first whiff told him what was wrong. He sat the extinguisher on the sidewalk. "Did you guys just fill up?" he asked.

"Yeah," George said, fanning the air. "Bad gas, you think?"

"Those aren't gas fumes," Felix said. "That's diesel."

Maria grabbed the receipt from her purse. Sure enough, George had filled her brand new Mustang with diesel fuel. "Oh, no-o-o-o!" she moaned.

Felix laughed. "Don't worry."

For the next hour he siphoned the diesel fuel from the Mustang's tank, cleaned the carburetor, then siphoned unleaded gas from his own car back into the Ford. "It'll smoke a little while longer. But it'll be okay."

From that moment on, Maria counted Felix Serna among her most cherished friends—and she never let George pump gas again.

Limited in the types of entertainment they could enjoy together—movies and television weren't options—George and Maria spent long hours listening to rock music or singing together while George strummed the guitar. She tried to teach him the lyrics to their favorite folk songs in Spanish, but finally gave up. Like Carlos before her, she accepted at last that he was Hispanic only in name, not in culture.

On other occasions, they would go to the small home Maria owned on nearby Idaho Street where she would cook his favorite meat-and-potatoes meals, then read to him from her well-stocked library. In addition to becoming reacquainted with his boyhood favorites, Faulkner, Steinbeck, and Hemingway, for the first time he became familiar with the works of Dostoyevsky, Tolstoy, Dickens, Cortazar, and Fuentes.

"If I'd had someone like you as a reader when I was in the university," he remarked one day, "I'd have made the honor roll."

"Uh-huh," she retorted, moving slightly out of range from what she knew was coming, "*if* you'd had someone like me to take the tests for you."

"Oh, yeah," he exclaimed, and tried, as he had on other occasions when she chided him, to take a swat at her behind. He never connected—unless she wanted him to.

One day, Maria arrived at the house before George got home. Cindi met her at the door. "I just made a fresh pot of coffee," she said.

"Sound's good," Maria replied. She settled into a chair at the kitchen table.

It was their first opportunity to speak alone. Cindi realized there was no need to express her affection for Maria. She had made that clear from the beginning, just as she had made clear the pleasure she took from watching George awaken to this new and important relationship in his life. But there was something on her mind. "Maria, has George ever mentioned running to you?"

"Oh, yes. He's told me all about his races."

"No, what I meant was, has he ever mentioned running *again*. He hasn't been doing that, you know, not since he came back from Holland. It was so much a part of his life before... well, what happened over there. He hasn't talked to me about it, but I think he misses it more than he lets on."

"No," Maria said, wondering why it hadn't occurred to her before this, "he hasn't mentioned that at all."

The following Saturday, Maria arrived at George's home wearing her running suit. "Dress out," she said. "I want to see the places where you used to run."

"Really?" he said.

"Really. Hurry up," she added, not wanting to give him an opportunity to think of a reason to decline. "I'll wait in the car."

Fifteen minutes later he came out of the house wearing the running gear he had stowed away in his closet the previous summer. He gave her directions to the back acres on Stahmann Farms. On the way, he told her about Phil Shapiro and the routine they worked out that eventually brought him the gold in the nationals.

That morning George and Maria made their first cross-country run together, through the pecan groves that had played such an important role in his past. They didn't get very far. Fifteen minutes into the run, George called for a stop. He dropped to the ground and leaned back against one of the trees.

"Man," he complained, gasping for breath, "you sure can... lose it... fast."

She sat down beside him, barely winded.

"Well, George Mendoza" she said, "from now on, I'm

just going to have to be your Phil Shapiro." And George discovered that he had a renewed interest in his old sport.

At least three times a week following that first outing, she would drive him to Stahmann Farms, or to the high mesa below the Organ Mountains, where they would run together while George rebuilt his legs and lungs. Soon, one mile became two, then two miles became four, until at last they were running seven to ten miles a day. For the first couple of months, she paced him. Thereafter, as his strength returned, he paced her. Through it all, she acted as his eyes, warning him of rocks, sudden changes in terrain, rattlers coiled near the trail.

One windy afternoon on the mesa, they pulled their jacket hoods tight against the blowing sand and took off on a five-mile run. About halfway through Maria found herself out in front, alone. She turned about quickly and retraced her steps. She found George standing beside the trail cursing at the top of his voice and throwing punches at the air.

"George, what's wrong?!"

"This bastard here ran into me, that's what's wrong. Now he won't let me pass."

The "bastard" was a six-foot-tall elk horn cactus with arm-like limbs that were thrashing wildly in the wind.

"I think this is a better day for reading," she said, and led him through the blinding dust back to the car.

He took delight in all the books she read to him, but his favorite was Hemingway's *The Sun Also Rises*. Often, between other readings, he would ask her to reread passages from it.

One evening she asked him why he was so captivated by the story.

"The love angle," he said. "Jake's a cripple, like me..."

She'd never heard him use that word before, and it upset her. "Don't say that," she said, heatedly.

"Okay. Jake was *impaired*... how's that?

"Anyway, he wasn't a whole person... a lot worse than me, really. Still, Lady Brett, who was a whole woman in every way, loved him, and never stopped loving him."

He paused. "Do you think a couple like that could be for real? I mean... a whole person, like you, and a disabled person like me? Making a go of it in the real world, together?"

This time she moved closer to him rather than farther away. "Yes, Mr. Mendoza," she said. "I think something like that is quite for real."

It wasn't their first kiss. But this embrace sealed the reality they both had recognized for months. They were deeply in love.

Often, on the days they went to the mesa, Maria would fix sandwiches and lemonade. After running, they would find a table in one of the picnic areas, have dinner, then stay to watch the sunset. Although George couldn't see the larger scene, he could detect colors in the high mountain air not visible to him elsewhere. By now they were comfortable sharing their innermost thoughts. One day, as they picnicked in the shade of a ponderosa grove, he began to talk about the afternoon he had spent in the park in Belgium, after his appointment with Dr. Francois. He told her he had remained there for hours, pondering the accomplishments of the disabled athletes in the Olympiad in Holland. How the feats he had witnessed were not celluloid fantasies, but genuine triumphs of the spirit. How European fans had come by the thousands to cheer athletes who were virtually ignored in America. How he had dreamed of being able to do something to change that—of finding a way to chronicle the triumphs of the handicapped athletes in America, as they were chronicled in Europe.

"But that's a torch someone else will have to pick up," he lamented. "It'll happen some day. But it ended for me in Holland."

"Why?" she asked. "Because of one stupid race?"

"I'm afraid it was more than that," he said, with a note of contrition. "I wasn't exactly a true-blue team player over there. I got kicked out of the village, remember?"

"So? You made a mistake. If you let that stop you, you're not the guy I think you are. I know you pretty well, George Mendoza. You can do anything you set your mind to."

"I can't repair watches."

"Quit quibbling. You know what I mean."

He leaned over and kissed her. "Thank you for saying it, anyway." Then he grasped her by the shoulders and turned her to face the opposite direction. "What do you see?"

"What do you mean?"

"Up high. I can't see it, but I know it's there. What do you see."

"You mean the Organs?"

"Yeah. Baylor Pass is up there. I ran in that race a couple of times. Last time I came in dead last, and I wasn't as blind then as I am now. You say I can do anything I set my mind to. Do you think I could run the Baylor Pass again?"

She gave an involuntary shudder. "That's not fair. I wouldn't even want you to try."

He pulled her back to him and held her close with her head on his shoulder. "And you're right."

They sat in silence, watching the crazy quilt of brilliant hues play across the desert sky. After awhile, Maria asked, "George, what you told me about Chimayo—what happened to you there, do you think you may have been hallucinating? I've heard people say that."

"Or that I fell asleep from exhaustion and dreamed it, or that I was on dope, or drunk. I've heard it all. But I'm the one who was there. I *know* what happened."

"Do your honestly believe God spoke to you?"

"I've never doubted it."

"Do you think you accomplished everything He wanted you to do?"

"No, but I gave it my best shot. I don't think He'll hold it against me."

After a while, she said. "George, let's make a deal. What are..."

"Now you sound like a game show host," he broke in.

She slapped him on the leg. "Be serious."

"Ow... that hurt!" He rubbed his leg. "Okay, I'm serious. What deal?"

"What are your chances of being picked for the Olympiad team in 1984?"

He let out a guffaw. "After the way I screwed up in Holland? About as much chance as being picked for astronaut training."

Warming to the subject, she sat up and looked directly at him. "Okay, let's put it to the test. You keep on training. I'll keep running with you... mark your times for you."

"That's the deal?"

"No. The deal is this: if you get picked for the 1984 Olympiad team, it means God wants you to get on with your dream of becoming a catalyst for the handicapped. If you're not picked, then we'll just get on with our life together and never mention it again."

"You're serious, aren't you?"

"I'm serious. What do you say?"

Had it not been for what happened to him years before

in Chimayo he would have laughed at the idea. He knew better than that now. Also, he loved Maria too much to ridicule her suggestion. "Okay. What's to lose?"

They sealed the pact with a kiss.

Chapter
25

Two years from the time they met at their mutual friends' wedding in San Miguel, George John Mendoza and Maria del Rosario Escobedo were married in a simple civil ceremony in Las Cruces. Attending were Maria's parents, George's grandparents and mother, and his one-time running guru, Phil Shapiro, and his wife. The civil ceremony was a deference Maria, a Catholic, made to George's sensibilities about denominations. Although deeply religious, he refused to categorize his concept of God with a specific dogma.

As a wedding gift, family and friends treated the new bride and groom to a honeymoon at *The Inn of the Mountain Gods*, in the heart of the Mescalero Apache Indian reservation in southern New Mexico. To George, the days he spent at the enchanting resort with Maria, hiking forest trails, sailing the azure lake, or just sitting on the balcony while Maria described the dance of sundown shadows on snow-capped Sierra Blanca peak were the happiest of his life.

Often during those memorable first days of their marriage, George would reflect on the role fate had played in his life. What if his mother hadn't read about El Santuario de Chimayo? What if T. G. Gibbs' untimely death hadn't moved him to visit the little chapel a second time? What if Ruben Sandoval hadn't been there to encourage him and provide the shelter and food that enabled him to remain for that third momentous day? What if Ernie Barge hadn't invited him to go to the wedding at San Miguel? What if Cindi hadn't encouraged him to change his mind after he turned Ernie down? What if Maria had been sitting ten rows ahead of him instead of one?

Fate, coincidence, or destiny? He pondered the question. Whichever, he concluded, he knew that his hope of finding a woman to love, and to love him, had been fulfilled beyond his fondest expectation. He vowed to make himself worthy of her trust.

Following the honeymoon, George moved from the home he shared with his mother on Baldwin Street into Maria's smaller home on Idaho Street. As soon as he was resettled, he kept his promise to Maria by undertaking a spirited training program.

Assuming the role once played by Phil Shapiro, Maria became her husband's new running guru. Side-by-side they began twice-a-week cross-country runs on the mesa where George had trained with the New Mexico Aggies. Other days, they practiced the 1,500-meter race at Stahmann Farms.

Following the Olympiad in Holland, George had begun to harbor doubts about the tactic Phil taught him about holding back to save energy for the final lap. It had worked in the USABA nationals, but it had lost him the gold in Arnhem. He expressed his misgivings to Maria.

"It wasn't Phil's tactic that lost in Holland," she countered. "It was *your* tactic. You've never raced the clock, you've always raced the person ahead of you. From now on, when you go into your final kick, run like there's *always* someone ahead of you."

He laughed. "You know, Coach Morgan could use someone like you on his staff."

"I've got all the runners I care to deal with right here," she retorted.

In January 1982, George verbally petitioned USABA Region 8 officials for authorization to reenter USABA track and field events. Despite the record of his impropriety in Holland—a story that had circulated throughout USABA—his petition was approved. At the first meet that spring, held in March in Austin, Texas, he took the silver in both the 1,500-meter and the 800-meter races. Although they were second-place showings, the races renewed George's faith that he could still compete in USABA events, even though many of the athletes he now faced were years younger than he.

Early that summer, after an invigorating run at Stahmann Farms, Maria sat resting with her back against one of the trees and patted the ground for George to sit beside her. When he did, she reached over and took his hand. "You're going to have to run by yourself for a while."

"How come?" he asked. "We make a pretty good pair out here."

"We've been more than 'a pair' for some time now."

It took him a moment. Then: "You're pregnant." It was a simple statement, void of passion.

She nodded, and he was close enough to see the radiant happiness in her face.

He laid his head back against the tree and closed his eyes. "Oh, boy," he sighed.

"Hey, don't fret about it. I'll still tag along to clock your times."

He didn't respond.

His reaction took her by surprise. She hadn't expected him to shout with joy or dance among the trees. That wasn't his style. Still, she had expected him to show some emotion. "George, are you unhappy about this?"

He gave her hand a squeeze. "Unhappy? No, of course not. It's just... well, it's gonna mean a big change in our lives."

"We'll do okay," she reassured him.

And that's how she passed off his faint disclaimer, as a big change in his life that would take time for him to fully understand and adjust to.

Michael George Mendoza was born at Las Cruces Memorial Hospital on October 25, 1982. That evening when Cindi went to visit her new grandson, George was sitting in a chair he'd moved to a corner of the room away from the bed. He was staring into the mid-distance, unaware that his mother was there. She stepped over and took him by the arm and led him to the bed, where Maria was once again checking her baby's body parts to make sure they were all there.

Cindi chuckled at the sight. "That's always the first thing a new mother does."

She looked lovingly at Michael, than up at George. "Someday," she said, "he will be your eyes."

The look that crossed George's countenance at that moment sent an icy tremor through Cindi. She hoped that Maria, absorbed with Michael, hadn't noticed. George returned to his chair without comment.

Something was terribly wrong, and Cindi thought she knew what it was. She'd meant to stay only a short while, to leave early so the new family could get acquainted with each other. Instead, she pulled a chair to the bedside and kept Maria company through the evening.

At the announcement signaling the end of visiting hours, Cindi kissed Maria and Michael, then turned to George. "How do you intend to get home?"

"Felix brought me. He said to call when I'm ready."

"I'll take you," she said.

"Nah, that's okay."

"*I'll take you,*" Cindi insisted.

George shrugged. "If that's what you want."

There was an eerie silence in the car as Cindi drove across town that night. Usually when she took George home after dark she would park so the headlights would focus on the house to give him a lighted pathway to the door. This time when she stopped she turned off the lights and the engine.

"I think we should talk," she said.

"What about?"

"You're worried about Michael's eyesight, aren't you?"

"Whatever gave you that idea? We've talked to the doctors. They say the odds are so much in his favor that we shouldn't even think about it."

"Well, something's wrong. You're certainly not yourself. You haven't been since Maria got pregnant."

He made no comment.

"Why don't you tell me what's bothering you?" she said. "Maybe I can help."

"What's to tell?" he snapped in an angry tone.

He opened the car door and started to get out. Then he hesitated and turned back to her. "Look, I didn't mean to jump all over you. It's just, well... what the hell am I supposed to do now? What do I know about being a father? I didn't exactly have a sterling role model in that department, you know."

He got out and shut the door. She turned the headlights on. Seconds later, he disappeared into the house.

She sat there for a long while, plagued by a sense of guilt, wondering what she should have said. No words came to mind. She looked toward the house. "I'm so sorry," she uttered into the darkness. Then she started the car and drove away.

In the weeks that followed, George virtually shunned his son. Maria was prepared for it. The day following Cindi's first visit, she returned to the hospital and told Maria about the scene in front of the house the night before. Both women decided it was a passing phase, that George would soon adjust. Given the circumstances of his upbringing, it would just take longer for him than it did for other new fathers.

They were wrong.

Instead of adjusting, George grew ever more detached from Michael. Whenever Maria asked him to do something that required hands-on contact with the baby, there was always something else he had to do. He began to spend long hours in seclusion with his Visualtek, reading books and magazines he had never cared for before. Not once since his wife and baby returned from the hospital had he gone running. Stranger yet—even dangerous—he began to take long walks alone at night, often not returning until after Maria had gone to bed. On those occasions, unless there was a bright moon, he was essentially totally blind. Only his encyclopedic knowledge of the streets of Las Cruces kept him from harm.

Though her patience was wearing thin, Maria vowed to tolerate her husband's aberrant behavior for as long as it took for him to come to his senses. Then, the day after Thanksgiving, her tolerance came to an abrupt end.

She was cooking noodles that afternoon that she intended to use in a turkey casserole that evening. She had just carried the boiling pot to the sink to drain when Michael let out a cry from his crib in the back bedroom. He had been colicky all that day and she had just gotten him down for a nap a few minutes before. George was in the living room listening to his favorite country-western station on the radio.

"George!" she called from the kitchen. "Get Michael, please. I've got my hands full."

"He'll be okay," George called back.

Another sharp cry came from the crib.

Frustrated, Maria turned to set the pot down. The bottom of the pan caught the edge of the counter, and noodles and boiling water spilled out across the kitchen floor. Only a quick step backward kept her from being scalded.

"Damn it!" she yelled, and threw the pot on the floor with the rest of the mess.

She ran to the bedroom and found that Michael had vomited. She wiped his face then picked him up and burped him until he passed some of the trapped gas. Then she cleaned him up, sat in her rocker, and rocked him until he grew quiet.

All the while, the twangy music from the radio came blaring back from the living room. She could bear it no longer. She carried Michael to the living room, went to the couch where George was sitting, and switched off the radio. She held their son out to him.

"Hold him," she said.

He gave her a curious side glance. "You know I'm no good at that."

"Hold him!" she demanded.

Startled by the sharp command, he instinctively put out his hands. She released Michael to him. He held his son at arms length, absolutely bewildered about what to do next.

"That is Michael George Mendoza," she said, her voice like steel. "He is your son. He is your flesh and blood. He is your responsibility... and he *needs* you."

He started to lay Michael on the couch beside him, but she took the baby and sat in a nearby chair. George folded his arms across his chest and grasped his shoulders. He was trembling.

"*Madre de Dios*, George, look at you. You're trying to hide within yourself. Can't you understand what's going on here? Can't you see the ghost that's come between us... ever since you learned I was pregnant?"

"Ghost?" he said, hoarsely.

"You complain to anyone who'll listen how you grew up without a father. Can't you see that's precisely what's happening to your own son? You're obsessed with a shadow from the past. You've let the bitterness you've harbored all these years poison you against fatherhood. It's destroying you, it's destroying all of us. *It cannot go on.*"

From the look on his face, she knew she had struck a raw nerve. He remained on the couch, rigidly still, for several minutes. At last he rose and went to the bedroom. When he came back he was carrying his sleeping bag and canteen. "I'm going out."

"I thought you would."

"Don't wait up for me."

"I never do, anymore."

He started for the door.

"George."

He turned around.

"I know where you're going. There's something else you should think about while you're out there. God opened doors for you that you thought were closed forever. He gave you a dream when all you had before was nightmares. If the dream dies in you now, it dies forever."

He looked at her for a moment, then turned and left without another word.

The following afternoon she was preparing Michael for his bath when she heard George enter the house. She went on about her business. She had just placed the baby on the bathinette when George stepped up to her side.

"Can I do that?" he asked.

She knew better than to make a big thing of it.

"Sure." She handed him the washcloth. "I'll go fix you something to eat."

"Good. I'm starving."

She watched from the doorway for a moment, just to make sure he knew what he was supposed to do. He was proceeding reasonably well. With a lighter heart, she went to the kitchen to fix sandwiches and tea, leaving her husband and son to get acquainted with each other—at last.

Chapter
26

Throughout that sleepless night George spent in his private hideaway on the mesa, he had agonized over yet another low ebb in his life. Where, he had wondered, was the guidance he prayed for in El Santuario following his return in disgrace from Holland?

Recounting that dark, all-night ordeal in later conversations with family and friends, George recalls his ire that Maria's searing rebuke kept interfering with his pipeline to God. No sooner would he send up another prayer, than his mind would be filled by her voice: *If the dream dies in you now, it dies forever.*

It was well after dawn, while he was washing in the icy stream below the hideaway, that the profound truth of that night struck him with the force of a thunderbolt. Standing there with cold water dripping from his body, he realized that he had been as blind in spirit as he was in sight! Maria's haunting words were not an impediment to his prayer for guidance. They were the *answer* to that prayer.

As clearly as if he had received instructions from Mount Sinai, he knew at last what he must do. Maria had seen the truth. He *was* obsessed with a ghost from the past—with the crippling longing for a father who had never been and would never be. He would never be able to exorcise that pain from his life completely. But he could damn well make sure that never again would it come between him and his family.

Three hours later, after a quick-paced walk from the mesa, he arrived home to find Maria preparing Michael for his bath. When he offered to help, he made the first move toward becoming a full-time father.

Over the sandwiches she fixed that day, he told her what had happened at the hideaway. Then he reached for her hand. "There'll be no ghost between us from now on. I promise you that."

Literally overnight, George underwent a transformation from a hands-off parent to one who shared every chore. He bathed Michael, changed his diapers, rocked him to sleep, burped him after meals, pushed his stroller or carried him in a papoose sling when they went for walks.

When he resumed running, Michael went along. On the days they went to the mesa or to Stahmann Farms, Maria would lay a quilt on the ground and sit with Michael while George went through his training routines. As she had promised she would, she continued to clock his times, recording them in a daily diary so they could note his progress. Though he never again matched his record-setting times in the USABA Nationals, or even in Holland, he was well within the qualifying times for the upcoming 1984 Olympiad, now scheduled to be held in New York.

He still considered his chances for being selected to compete in that event to be the longest of long shots. Past teammates had shared with him the rumor that his expulsion from the 1980 team had soured some USABA members against his being considered for the 1984 team, regardless of his qualifications. The pact he made with Maria centered on his being picked for the team. They had agreed to accept it as a sign that he was to get on with his dream of becoming a catalyst for the handicapped. Now, he considered that criterion passé. God had spoken loud and clear the morning George was bathing in an icy stream on the mesa: *If the dream dies in you now, it dies forever.*

God had not waited for the USABA selection committee to make up its mind. And neither would George.

Late one afternoon he came home with four books he had checked out of the university library: *Writing TV and Movie Scripts That Sell, Film and Television Handbook, A Guide to the Screen Writers Guild, Index to Contemporary Authors.*

For the next week, spending every spare hour at the task, he read through each volume at his Visualtek. It was laborious, line-by-line work. When he finished, he had the names of scores of script writers, directors, producers, cinematographers, actors, authors, and agents who had been connected with the writing, production, or promotion of books or films on inspirational subjects—athletics preferred. Enlisting Maria's skills as a typist, he created a form letter defining his ideas for an educational film based on USABA-promoted sporting events, designed to awaken viewing audiences and the media to the courage and accomplishment of physically disabled American athletes. He mailed a copy of the letter to every person on his list, to the New Mexico

Film Commission, to each member of the New Mexico congressional delegation, to the major television networks, and to the CEOs of major corporations he felt might be interested in sponsoring the project. It was the beginning of one of the most quixotic crusades ever undertaken by a would-be movie promoter.

"Do you believe it'll work?" Maria asked when they dropped the final batch of letters in the mailbox.

"If not this year, maybe next year. If not next year, maybe the year after. However long it takes, I'll be ready."

On October 25, 1983, Cindi and Aunt Linda came to dinner to help George and Maria celebrate Michael's first birthday. The banter around the table was jovial. Linda regaled the gathering with the tale of the afternoon she let George drive her International Scout on the mesa.

"And she was foolish enough to let him do it again," Cindi piped in.

"Well, sure," Linda countered. "It's the best way I've found to lose weight."

When the laughter died, Linda asked, "How about you, Maria? Do you ever let George drive your Mustang?"

"No way!" Maria exclaimed. "And I'll never let him put gas in it again, either!"

And she delighted them with that story.

Later in the evening over cake and ice cream, George made an unexpected announcement. "The Baylor's coming up in twenty-five days. I've decided to enter." He said it as casually as if he were talking about a trip to the supermarket.

At once, the lighthearted mood of the evening turned sour. Maria was sitting at the table beside George. Cindi had pushed her chair back and was holding Michael. The two women exchanged troubled glances.

Maria spoke first. "You told me you weren't going to do that again."

"When did I tell you that?"

"That day on the mesa, when we made our pact. You made me look up at the Organs, and I said I wouldn't want you to try to run Baylor Pass again. You said I was right."

"And she *was* right," Cindi spoke up. "You could see better when you ran the Baylor before. And you almost broke you neck. Anyway, you're too late. The deadline for registration was last week."

"Registration is for people who want their time entered

in the record books. I don't care about that."

The more they tried to argue with him, the more obdurate he became.

"But why?" Maria asked, in exasperation. "You've got the whole mesa at your disposal, you're running well at Stahmann. That's all the training you need to qualify for the Olympiad. Why the Baylor all of a sudden?"

"This isn't about the Olympiad," he replied. "It's about the Baylor. And it's because it *is* the Baylor. I can't explain it any better than that. And it's not all of a sudden. I've been thinking about it for months. I just know it's something I have to do one more time before I hang it up. You understand, don't you Aunt Linda?"

Linda raised a hand in protest. "Just leave me out of this one."

George put his arm around Maria. "I'd like to think you'll be there at the finish line, waiting for me."

She shook her head in frustration. "George Mendoza, you're one obstinate *bastardo*, you know that?"

"Sure, I do. Does that mean you'll be there?"

"Where else?" she replied. "I'll bring plenty of bandages."

He laughed.

No one else did.

Chapter
27

In the predawn hours of Sunday, November 19, 1983, George was awakened by a strange sound coming from his own throat. The side of the bed where he lay was drenched with sweat. He sat bolt upright and reached out his hand toward Maria. She was lying still, breathing easily. Good. He had suppressed the scream before it awakened her, too.

The nightmare was still vivid in his mind. It was the same horrifying dream he'd had as a child on Long Island after he got lost in an impenetrable fog and slipped off a perilous forest trail. On that long-ago night, he had dreamed he was going blind. Cindi had comforted him, assuring him that all was well, that nightmares don't come true.

Now, he picked up the oversize LED digital clock he kept on the nightstand and moved the lighted numerals close to his face. It was 4:30 a.m. He kicked back the covers and sat up on the edge of the bed. He didn't need a degree in psychology to interpret this night's dream. His blindness was no longer fantasy. The nightmare of his youth had come true. He was trapped forever in an impenetrable fog, and another perilous trail awaited him this morning. For this was the day of the 13th Annual Baylor Pass Race—just five and one-half hours from now.

He got up and pulled on his robe and went to the dining room. Mounted beside a painting of *The Last Supper*, which Maria had hung on the wall above the table soon after they were married, was a smaller case holding the medals he had won over the years. He took down the case and placed it on the table. Then he sat down and took out the medals and ran his fingers over them, recognizing each from some distinctive marking on the face or the ribbon. There were golds from Macomb, Seattle, and Missoula. There were silvers from Macomb, Austin, Canada, and St. Louis. There was no bronze, and no medal at all from Arnhem, Holland.

He thought back to the night of Michael's first birthday, when he had surprised—shocked was a better word—his mother and Maria when he announced that he intended to run the Baylor again. He had tried to explain that it was something he had to do. From their reaction he knew he hadn't mollified them. After awhile he quit trying. He knew of no words that would make them feel the burning need that gnawed at him to prove to the world that Arnhem was not his legacy; that the boy from Centereach—the kid "with glue on his fingers" whom the sportswriters once hailed as having pro potential—was still a force to contend with. The need to do it before it all came to an end—as he knew it must, soon.

He was still reminiscing when he heard Maria get up to attend to Michael. Was it that late? He glanced toward the window and saw that the sun was up. He went to the kitchen, where Maria was heating baby food.

"I've been up a while," he said.

"I know. You want tea and toast?" Her tone told him that she still wasn't reconciled to what they faced this day.

She had offered his usual race-day breakfast. Instead, thinking about the large helping of pasta he'd eaten last night, he asked, "Is there any macaroni left?"

"Yes. Want it heated?"

"Uh-uh."

And that's what he ate that morning of the 13th Annual Baylor Pass Race. Cold macaroni and cheese.

Since harrier Al Rodney made history by winning the first Baylor Pass Race in August 1971 in a field of twenty-one runners, the event had experienced unabated growth. Of the 250-plus people who gathered in the foothills of the Organ Mountains for the Baylor that November day, 172 were officially entered in the race. It was one of the largest fields in Baylor history. At 9:00 a.m., Maria drove George to the west slope of the Organs, where the race would begin. He got out, decided that his two-piece, cool-weather running suit was all he needed, and threw his jacket back in the car. Maria gave him a kiss for luck, then drove to the Aguirre Springs recreation area on the east slope, the finish line. Among the crowd already gathered there were Cindi (holding Michael), Aunt Linda, Felix Serna, and several of George's classmates from NMSVH and NMSU.

After Maria parked and joined the family, Felix checked his watch. It was 9:45 a.m. "Fifteen minutes," he said. There was nothing to do now but wait.

On the other side of the mountain, Coach Art Morgan,

who, along with his wife, Anne, was now a major force in keeping the annual Baylor event alive and well, shouted orders through his bullhorn to assemble the runners at the starting line. To avoid gridlock at the outset, the fastest runners, based on past records, were positioned in the front. Slower runners, first-time entrants, and unofficial participants were positioned in the rear. Because of the growing field of runners in recent years, entrants were grouped by gender and age. Men were grouped into five age categories: 17 and under, 18 to 29, 30 to 39, 40 to 49, and 50 and over. Women were grouped into four age categories: 17 and under, 18 to 29, 30 to 39, and 40 and over. Despite this, all runners started at the same time. The different categories were established so that awards could be presented to winners in each group. Coach Morgan was both race starter and timekeeper. As soon as he fired the starting gun, he would run to his car and make the half hour drive around the mountain to Aguirre Springs, usually arriving no sooner than ten minutes before the first runner crossed the finish line.

At the "crack!" of the gun that morning, the runners took off en masse on the long first leg up the west face of the Organs. Within minutes, the congestion had dispersed to an extended string of runners vying for position along a trail barely wide enough for two to run side by side.

At the rear of the pack, George, an unofficial entrant, loped along at a slow pace. The day was cloudy, bright, with enough sun falling on the trail for him to distinguish the bare, well-beaten path from the rougher terrain on each side. Years before, he had walked every inch of the Baylor, memorizing its features. Now, the course unfolded before him in his mind, like a programmed map scrolling down a computer screen. Sticking to the routine Phil Shapiro had taught him during their training days together, he conserved his energy for the demanding four-mile uphill leg that lay directly ahead, and the final downhill sprint to come.

At the base of the incline he was still holding pace in the rear. Then, as the grade steepened into the first of many grueling switchback turns to come, he began to pass slower runners. He took no heart in it, realizing that those falling behind this early were older or inexperienced runners. He maintained his slow, steady pace.

As he neared the summit, his legs started to burn, just as

they had done the last time he attempted this punishing race, when he finished dead last. Within minutes, his thighs were on fire. The 6,000-foot crest lay just ahead. He sucked in deep breaths to counter the dwindling oxygen supply at the higher altitude. He knew he would top out soon.

Moments after he reached the summit, he heard a yell from ahead, accompanied by the unmistakable thud of someone falling on the trail. To have heard the fall so clearly, George realized he had to be near to the victim. He judged the sounds as having come from the right side of the track. Trying to avoid a collision, he shifted to the left. It was a mistake. The sight of a man scrambling to regain footage appeared in George's vision—dead ahead. Unable to dodge, George struck him with such force that both went tumbling down a rocky embankment.

At the bottom of the gully, the man jumped to his feet again. "Hey, fellow," he barked, "keep your damned eyes open or get off the track!"

The man took off again, leaving George where he lay.

Rising on his hands and knees, George clawed his way back to the trail and picked up the pace. In his peripheral vision, he saw people jumping out of his way. They were running toward him!

"Look out!" someone yelled.

"Turn around!" another voice shouted.

Just then someone grabbed him by the arm. "Wrong way, Mendoza!" a feminine voice said. She swung him around in his tracks and gave him a hard slap on his butt. "Get cracking!"

To this day, George does not know the identity of his benefactor at that crucial moment, although she obviously knew him. One clue: she had "a mighty powerful swat."

He figured he had lost a full precious minute. Forsaking caution, he abandoned his conservative pace, fixed his eyes on the rim of the trail, and started again in a furious sprint. Negotiating the switchbacks by dim vision and memory, he began to pass runners. One... a couple... a half dozen. Now into the east-face descent, he calculated that he was somewhere near the lead of perhaps the last fifty runners in the pack. Well over a hundred remained ahead.

Winning the Baylor had never entered his mind. Finishing was his cherished goal. It had been eleven years, almost to the day, since he had amazed friends and coaches alike at

NMSVH by winning his first-ever race, despite the fiasco of tripping over his shorts half-way through. Now, those elapsed years, plus his on-again off-again training routine, were taking their toll. Already, runners who had exhausted their stamina sat with their heads bent forward on their knees or lay prone on the wayside. A couple were sucking on oxygen bottles hurriedly brought by spotters. Some, unable to make it down the mountain on their own, would have to be helped.

Contrary to lay belief, the downhill segment of a distance race can be more demanding than the uphill segment. Muscles are screaming, lungs are bursting, yet the runner must exert near-superhuman effort to remain erect on legs that must keep up a steady pace as well as maintain an awkward, back-leaning balance against the pull of gravity. Historically, more harriers falter on the downhill than on the uphill.

And George was beginning to falter.

Long before the midway point of the final descent he felt his legs start to wobble. It was a sure sign that he was near collapse. He weighed options. Although he couldn't see it, he knew that the finish line was less than two miles ahead. He could try to maintain the pace in hopes of finishing in the last 10 percent of the field, he could slow the pace and cross the finish line last or near last—but at least finish—or he could quit. Lungs, heart, and muscles cried out for him to end the punishment. In eleven years of competitive running, he had never quit a race. The mere thought of doing so now was agony. But reality was reality. He started to ease to the side of the trail.

At that moment the path, the air, and the sky around him became illuminated by a light so bright that it startled him. Almost simultaneously, he realized what was happening. He was experiencing a phenomenon not uncommon to those who happen to be in the right spot at the right time in certain mountains in southern New Mexico.

On the floor of the Tularosa Basin, just below Baylor Peak, White Sands National Monument forms a 230-square-mile alabaster expanse bracketed by the Organ and Sacramento Mountains. Driven by desert winds, fifty-foot-high gypsum dunes constantly shift position in a slow but relentless march northward. Visitors who tour the monument soon learn that sunglasses with extra-dark tint are imperative to protect their eyes from the sun's rays reflecting off the sand with dazzling intensity. At certain times of the day, these radiant reflections can be seen from miles away. Such was the case that morning when George happened to be running in the exact location down the east face of the Organ Mountains to be enveloped by a reflection from White Sands.

So much for the rational explanation.

The reality to George at that awesome moment was that once again he was running toward the light. A vision of his beloved El Santuario filled his mind. A renewal of energy surged through his body. Willing throbbing muscles to superhuman effort, he kicked into the final high-prancing sprint that had brought him glory at Macomb, Seattle, and Missoula. One by one, front-runners fell behind as he passed them by.

At Aguirre Springs, Coach Art Morgan arrived to join others at the officials' table near the finish line. His wife, Anne, was prepared to record the race results on the tally sheet. Within minutes after Coach Morgan's arrival, Simon Gutierrez, a student at Del Norte High School in Albuquerque, crossed the line with a winning time of 40:36. Other front-runners followed in close order.

Seated at a picnic table with George's family, Felix Serna stood on the seat and focused his binoculars on the peak.

"Has he topped out yet?" Maria asked, her voice apprehensive.

"I don't see him," Felix replied.

He started to sit. On second thought, he lowered the glasses to the string of runners who had already bottomed out and were sprinting toward the finish line.

"Good Lord!" he whooped.

He pulled Maria up beside him and handed her the glasses. She focused where he pointed and let out a yell. "George!"

Felix knew that at the pace George was running he would overshoot the finish line. He jumped down and ran to the line, arriving just as George crossed, without slowing. Felix caught up with George, grabbed him by the shoulders and pulled him to one side. George fell into Felix's arms, then sank to the ground, exhausted.

While Maria and Cindi attended to George, Felix went to the table where the Morgans were timing the finishers. He knew George's time wouldn't be listed, but he recognized the man who crossed the line just before him. He located the man's name and the time—56:16—60th position. George had finished in 61st position. He had defeated 112 *sighted* runners!

Felix hurried to the picnic table, where Maria and Cindi had just lowered George onto the seat. She was cleaning abrasions on his face and hands with a washcloth. His heavy running suit had protected him from other injuries during his fall from the trail. Felix gave them the exciting news.

Though still gasping for breath, George cried out: "All right!"

After a moment, in lowered voice, he said, "I sure wish T. G. could have been here to see it."

"Maybe he is," Maria said.

"Yeah," George said. "Maybe he is."

In years to come, George would claim that his accomplishment at the Baylor Pass Race that day meant more to him than winning the gold in Holland.

When at last George had recuperated, Cindi rose with Michael in her arms. "Let's all meet at the Sagebrush Inn in an hour," she suggested. "Celebration luncheon. My treat."

"What time is it now?" Maria asked.

Felix looked at his watch. Before he could reply, George stood. "I'll tell you what time it is."

He took Michael from his grandmother's arms, then pulled Maria to his side. Beaming with confidence and a renewed feeling of self-worth, he hugged his wife and child and exclaimed: "It's time to let the dream begin."

Afterword

In the years following his riveting performance at Baylor Pass in 1983, the milestones of George Mendoza's career underscore his indefatigable drive to achieve his twin goals of bringing about national recognition for handicapped athletes, and of aiding, teaching, and counseling any handicapped person, athlete or not.

A brief chronology:

In the spring of 1984, the United States Association of Blind Athletes astonished some, but pleased many, by selecting George to represent the United States at the 1984 Olympics for the Physically Disabled. That June, at Hofstra University in Uniondale, New York, near his Long Island home of Centereach, George competed in his last international meet. Running in his specialty, the 1,500-meter race, he crossed the finish line, as he had in Holland, in fourth place. But far from reacting as the dispirited young man who stalked away from the playing fields in Holland in anger, the former world champion considered New York a triumph. Just to be chosen to compete again was a victory in itself. Moreover, the honor he felt in being allowed to associate one last time with outstanding athletes from around the world, was reward enough for a lifetime.

In keeping with the pact he made with Maria on that courtship day on the mesa, George continued his letter-writing campaign to film producers, directors, writers, TV networks, and corporations regarding the need to awaken American audiences to the courage and accomplishments of physically disabled athletes. In a follow-up to his initial correspondence, he wrote:

"I want to make films for parents who may have low expectations for their children who may be physically disabled; for teachers who may have problems relating to physically disabled students; for employers who may doubt a physically disabled employee's ability to perform well; and just for the public in general."

Intrigued by the message, as well as George's persistent promotion and gung-ho personality, addressees began to respond. Over time, the Charles E. Culpepper Foundation, Mountain Bell Telephone Company, El Paso Community Foundation, Frank E. Gannet Newspaper Foundation, Yates Petroleum Company, Ethicon, Inc., L'eggs Corporation, American Airlines, Sandia National Laboratories, Stahmann Farms, Inc., and numerous private and/or anonymous supporters replied offering funding and/or technical support for his film projects.

In 1983, George joined with veteran Hollywood film producer Frank Zuniga and director Karen House, an Academy Award nominee, to produce a fifteen-minute documentary film designed to counter misconceptions about visually impaired persons. The film is used by USABA as a promotional vehicle.

Following the birth of their daughter, Guadalupe, on July 20, 1984, at Cindi's suggestion, George and Maria swapped houses with Cindi, as her house was the larger and more suited to a family. To George, it was one more example of his mother's continuing selfless devotion to him and his family's welfare.

In 1987, under the auspices of the Adolph Coors Corporation, George worked with Producer/Director/Writer Kelly Hostetler in bringing about *The George Mendoza Story*, a twenty-seven minute educational film depicting George's personal triumph over adversity. George, Cindi, and Maria play themselves in the production. Hosted by actor Robert Duval and narrated by Paula Woodward, the film premiered in Albuquerque on June 5, 1989, and aired on PBS around the country throughout the fall of that year. It is widely used as an inspirational teaching medium in schools and churches in this country and abroad.

George has begun negotiation with the United States Department of the Interior, Bureau of Land Management, regarding a Recreation and Public Purpose application for land near Las Cruces. His hope is to convert a parcel of public lands into a recreational ranch for young people, with emphasis on training handicapped youth in the skills necessary to their future livelihood. In discussing the project, George says, "I've got my medals behind me. I want to help those kids, handicapped or not, who may be able to have medals in *their* future if they get a boost from someone who's been there."

On August 19, 1987, New Mexico Governor Garrey Carruthers appointed George a member of the Governor's Committee on the Concerns of the Handicapped, an appointment he still holds. Two years later, in recognition of George's "fulfillment of his responsibilities with integrity and dedication," the governor proclaimed October 1, 1989, as "George Mendoza Day."

From February 1985 to May 1993, George worked as the, coordinator of disabled student programs at New Mexico State University in Las Cruces, his alma mater. It is a role he cherished. As an advocate of the needs of all disabled students entering the school, he participated in establishing institutional policy toward the handicapped, identified each disabled student's special needs, provided readers and interpreters for their studies both on and off campus, and negotiated on their behalf with faculty members. One could seldom visit the campus at NMSU without seeing George somewhere on the grounds, or in the hallways, or in a classroom, advising students with various disabilities on how to cope with the rigors of college life that non-disabled students take for granted.

Each August, in keeping with the tradition of Chimayo, George makes a renewal pilgrimage to the little village in northern New Mexico where he received his life's blessing. Although Ruben Sandoval has moved away, George always visits the gift shop that was once Sandoval Store, to stand for a moment where he once sat at the counter, just "to be close" to his one-time benefactor. In El Santuario, he still takes the front seat near the large *candelabro* where he experienced the vision that changed his life. In speaking of that fateful day in 1974, he expresses his devotion to the special people, as well as this special place, in his life: "I found my strength in my mother; I found my wisdom in my wife; I found my soul in Chimayo."

Under the auspices of The Program Corporation of America, New York, George is much in demand as a speaker, receiving invitations from schools, churches, business groups, medical associations, and various other organizations throughout the country. He usually shows one or both of his films before taking the podium, then stresses to his audience:

"In many people, a handicap is as destructive as they

allow it to be. Although one may be a 'person with a handicap,' one need not succumb to being a 'handicapped person.'"

As a testimonial, he relates the story of his own life, an inspiring insight into one man's long journey from darkness back into the light.

A MESSAGE FROM THE PUBLISHER

I happen to be an avid runner myself, although the only time I win a trophy is when almost nobody else in my age group lines up. But like many people, I've wondered how I would do—in running, and in life—if I lost my sight. In my case, this could feasibly happen, because my mother was blind with glaucoma at age 80, and I certainly hope to be running competitively into my 90s. George Mendoza is my kind of a man. And his true story may be a metaphoric guide to me in the years ahead. I hope you enjoy this book and are as inspired by it as I have been.

W. R. Spence, M.D.
Publisher

*A*t WRS Publishing, we are only interested in producing books we can be proud of—books that focus on people and/or issues that enlighten and inspire, books that change lives for the better, either through the celebration of human achievement or the revelation of human folly. **Call us at 1-800-299-3366 for suggestions or for a free book catalog.**

WATCH FOR THESE RELATED TITLES:

BLIND COURAGE tells the remarkable story of Bill Irwin, the first blind man to thru-hike the 2,100-mile Appalachian Trail.

NO LIMITS is the inspiring story of Harry Cordellos, blind runner, skier, triathlete, and role model.

THERE'S ALWAYS A WAY is the story of Kevin Saunders, who was paralyzed in a grain-elevator explosion that killed 10 people. Fighting back against incredible odds, he discovered wheelchair athletics and is now a decathlon paralympic champion and motivational speaker.

CLIMBING BACK, The Story of Mark Wellman, Yosemite's incredible paraplegic ranger, who climbed El Capitan and Half Dome.

WRS
PUBLISHING

A Division of WRS Group, Inc.
Waco, Texas